Francis Bugg

Quakerism Withering, and Christianity Reviving

Or, a brief reply to the Quakers pretended vindication. In answer to a

printed sheet deliver'd to the Parliament.

Francis Bugg

Quakerism Withering, and Christianity Reviving
Or, a brief reply to the Quakers pretended vindication. In answer to a printed sheet deliver'd to the Parliament.

ISBN/EAN: 9783337410773

Printed in Europe, USA, Canada, Australia, Japan

Cover: Foto ©Lupo / pixelio.de

More available books at **www.hansebooks.com**

𝕼𝖚𝖆𝖐𝖊𝖗𝖎𝖘𝖒 𝖂𝖎𝖙𝖍𝖊𝖗𝖎𝖓𝖌,

AND

Chriſtianity Reviving.

OR,

A Br1ef Reply

TO THE

𝕼𝖚𝖆𝖐𝖊𝖗𝖘 Pretended Vindication.

In Anſwer to a Printed Sheet deliver'd to the

PARLIAMENT.

WHEREIN

Their Errors, both in Fundamentals and Circumſtantials, are further detected, and 𝕲. 𝖂𝖍𝖎𝖙𝖊𝖍𝖊𝖆𝖉 further unmask'd.

By an Earneſt Contender for the Chriſtian Faith,
Francis Bugg.

Licens'd, *March* 3. 169¾.

Becauſe I have called, and ye refuſed, I have
ſtretched forth my hand, and no man regarded:
I alſo will laugh at your calamity, and mock
when your fear cometh. Prov. 1. 24, 26.

LONDON:

Printed for the Author, and ſold by *J. Dunton*
at the *Raven* in the *Poultry*, and *J. Guillam* Bookſeller
in *Biſhopſgate-ſtreet*, 1694.

TO THE
Right Reverend Father in GOD
EDWARD,
Lord Bifhop of *Gloucefter*.

My Lord,

SINCE by Divine Providence, after my many Years Converfation with the Quakers, I heard the firft Sermon by a Publick Minifter in your Church, whereby my Underftanding was in great part cleared from thofe cloudy Mifts which·fell from the confufed Notions and uncertain Doctrines of the *Quakers*; I think my felf bound in Duty to return Publick Thanks to God for that his Providence and Token of his Efpecial Favour ; as alfo to his Servants, who labour in the Word and Doctrine, and for the fame (however defpifed by the Ignorant) are worthy of Double Honour. And having been concerned in Confcience to unveil the Teachers of the *Quakers*, who bring in *Damnable Herefies*, even denying the

A 2   Lord

The Epiſtle Dedicatory.

Lord that bought them; I preſumed to
preſent your Lordſhip with the enſuing
Diſcourſe, who, as you know how to re-
buke with all Authority ſuch as wilfully
maintain Errors, ſo you alſo know how to
bear with, and forbear, ſuch as through
Infirmity may unwillingly err. ‑ I therefore do moſt humbly offer what I have
wrote to your Lordſhips Peruſal, and ſhall
moſt willingly ſubmit to your Cenſure the
Matters therein contained: And if, for
want of Judgment in the Matters contro-
verted, I have wronged the *Quakers*, I
ſhall moſt willingly Retract, and make
them publick Reparation ; believing on
the other hand, that if they be found
guilty of the Errors charg'd, that your
Lordſhip will think it requiſite, that they,
under their Hands, make an ingenuous
Retractation, according to their Pretences
in their printed Works. I am,

My Lord,

Tour Lordſhips moſt humble,

and moſt obedient Servant,

Fra. Bugg.

THE
PREFACE.

READER,

PRovidence hath so attended me, as that a Friend of mine (beholding the Injustice of G. W. to me, and especially his Pervertions of the Truths asserted by me) have answered his Book falsely stiled Innocency triumphant, &c. by his Book stiled Some Animadversions, &c. so that I need say nothing in answer to it. As for his large Quotation out of my Book De Christianæ Libertate, it was some years before I left the Quakers, and which G. W. need not boast of, for it was levelled at the Usurpation of their Womens Meetings ; and it gave Them a sore Wound as well as G. W. who wrote in favour of them : And indeed the Matter was so well managed, and the Book so well wrote, the Time considered, as I am glad it was no worse ; though I am grieved to behold so much wrote by me without any mention of the Death and Sufferings of Christ, his Resurrection, Ascension, and the Benefits accrewing thereby to Mankind ; and the more to consider how many there are led Captive, as I once was, to the Antichristian Doctrine of the Quakers, for whose sake I have been concerned, and had not G. W. withstood our words, I do think there might have been a better Understanding than there has. For my part, I declare solemnly, no Man can pursue an Accommodation with more Sincerity than I have done : How have I wrote ! how have I woo'd and entreated

treated

treated, that we might have a meeting to sentence what was wrong, and to press after Truth! And when I came to London, November *last, before I printed the Sheet to the Parliament, I wrote to* G. W. *to come to me, that we might have a meeting, that so be and I might engage a Retractation if need were. And as this was pursuant to their own Proposal mentioned* p. 2. *so it might have had a good effect,* viz.

I being now in Town, if you will come to my Lodging you shall be welcome; if you will have an hours private Difcourfe, I will promife, if you will do the like, never to take notice of what paffes, or be both at liberty, which you pleafe: If we can agree on terms to have a meeting, with 6 or 8 of a fide, it may be a means to prevent farther Controverfie: If you do not think good to come to me, if you invite me to come to your Houfe, or any other place, I will, &c.

This I wrote before I printed the Sheet deliver'd to the Parliament, but he was fo far from confenting to what I propofed, that he gave me no anfwer to my Letter; and when I faw that, I knowing what they had done againft me, I thought it prudence, for my own prefervation as well as for a general Good, to keep up the Teft againft Quakerifm, *I mean the Oath; for tho' they fay,* W. Smith's *Catechifm,* p. 79. Queft. ' *And are you fo difpofed* ' *toward your Enemies, as that you cannot feek Re-* ' *venge,* &c? Anf. *Yes, that is the difpofition of* ' *our Nature, not to feek Revenge, though we do* ' *fuffer*

The Preface.

' *suffer Wrong, for the Revenging Nature is in the*
' *Fall ; but it is not so with us, whom God has*
' *redeemed,* &c. *I say, notwithstanding this pre-*
tended Innocency, I found the Quakers *so fallen,*
and so much unredeemed, that I should rather fall
into the Hands of Papists, *if they had power, for*
had they power, they would be as often in the Fall
as out of the Fall, as often in old Adam *as in their*
new, as often in the Unredeemed as the Redeemed
State ; so the best way is to keep up the Test : Keep
them out of Places of Trust and Government, and
then they can only bark, and shew their Teeth ;
—— Canes timidi vehementius latrant.

 But since such as revenge themselves are in the
Fall, then they are not in their Star, their Branch,
G. Fox ; *for he said,* He was (when living) in
a state beyond the First *Adam* that fell, and
in the state of the Second *Adam* that never
fell ; That his very Marriage was above the
state of the First *Adam* in his Innocency, in
the state of the Second *Adam* that never fell ;
and that he never fell nor changed ; that he
had power to bind and loose whom he pleased, *&c.* See The Quakers unmask'd, *p.* 27.
Surely then W. C. *and* G. W's *other Creatures was*
all in the Fall, and unredeemed ; out of G. Fox,
that never fell nor changed ; out of their Star ; out
of their Branch notwithstanding their idolizing his
Motions, his Travels, his Sufferings, and merito-
rious Labours, and Books printed and reprinted,
sent abroad and dispersed : but left G. W. *leave out*
the History of his Glorified State in the Reprint,
I may Recite it ; see The Examination and
Tryal of G. *Fox,* at *Lancaster* Assize, *&c.* p. 21.
           'And

The Preface.

‘ *And before I came to the Bar, I was moved to*
‘ *pray, that the Lord would confound their Envy;*
‘ *and the thundering Voice answer'd, I have glori-*
‘ *fied thee, and will glorifie thee again. And I*
‘ *was so filled full of Glory, that my Head and Ears*
‘ *was filled full of it: And that when the Trum-*
‘ *pet sounded, and the Judges came up again, they*
‘ *all appear'd as dead Men under me,* &c. G. Fox.
Alluding to John 12. 28. *&* 16. 14. *&* 17. 1.

Now *you that are Disciples to* G. W. *pray mea-*
sure the Truth of the printed History of G. Fox *his*
Travels; if you find his Glorified State fairly re-
lated, as it is in his Book above recited, you may
be assured there is some Truth in it ; if not, you
may without breach of Charity conclude the said
History a Romance, a partial Story, some true,
some false, some put in, some left out, pieced and
patched, mended and painted.

BOOKS *written by* Fra. Bugg.

1. DE *Christianæ Libertate.*
2. The painted Harlot both stript and whipt, *&c.*
3. Reason against Railing, *&c.*
4. Innocency Vindicated, *&c.*
5. The Quakers detected, *&c.*
6. Battering Rams against *New Rome, &c.*
7. One Blow more at *New Rome, &c.*
8. *New Rome* unmask'd, *&c.*
9. *New Rome* arraign'd, *&c.*
10. Quakerism Withering, *&c.* Besides a Letter to the
    Quakers ; and a Sheet to the Parliament, *&c.*

ERRATA.

PAge 3. lin. 12. dele *thing* ; p. 40. l. 9. for *never* read
seldom; p. 43. l. 27. for *recommended* r. *mentioned* ;
p. 52. l. 23. for 2 r. 20. p. 58. l. 27. for *Hen.* r. *John* ;
p. 71. l. 20. for *left* r. *weaker* ; p. 60. l. 14. for *they out*
r. *they cut.*

𝔔ua-

Quakerifm Withering,

BUT

Chriftianity Reviving.

The Introduction.

Courteous Reader,

THE main thing I intend is a Defence of my Sheet to the Parliament, from the Falfe Gloffes of *George Whitehead* in the Quakers pretended *Vindication*; and to fhew wherein I have offer'd to meet *George Whitehead*, to debate matters, wherein he fays I have wronged the Quakers; which I am not confcious of: And this I did, firft, in anfwer to his Challenge *p.* 4. *viz.* To make it appear before any fix, ten, or twelve competent Witneffes, which cannot be rationally thought to be Quakers, in regard they are Parties concerned. So likewife did I offer to debate the matter, when I allowed him to have Quakers, upon condition that what they could not Juftifie he fhould Retract ; which

B   is

is according to their Offer in like Cafes ; as
in the Epiftle in the front of *Edw. Burroughs's*
Works, *&c. viz.* 'And fo gladly would we
'be made manifeft to all the World, —That
'we may freely and cheerfully, four, ten,
'twenty, more or fewer of us, give as many
'of the wifeft and ableft of the Priefts and
'Profeffors a meeting for Difpute at any
'place, and for what time ; and let fuch,
'whether them or us, that cannot prove our
'felves to be of the True Church, ——but
'found in Error, *&c.* renounce all their Re-
'ligion, and confefs to all the World under
'their Hands, that they have been deceived.
'——And upon thefe, or any equal Terms,
'would we willingly engage *all*, or *any one*, of
'thefe Sects, *&c.* As in *New-Rome unmask'd,*
p. 2. the faid Challenge is by me then acce-
pted, and by G. *W.* in his *Effay, &c. p.* 7. rejected ; which alfo is *W. Penn's* method.
Again in my printed Sheet to the Parliament,
p. 2. I offer'd before ten or twelve impartial
Men, to produce every Book and Page which
I therein quoted : This I did then offer with
the Sheet in my Hand, and many Quakers
prefent, but none of them put me upon proof ;
but G. *W.* in his pretended *Vindication, p.* 4.
faid, 'I G. *W.* freely offer to make it appear,
'before *any fix*, *ten*, or *twelve* competent Wit-
'neffes, who are moderate Men of Sence and
'Reafon, that F. *B.* has grofly abufed and
'perverted Truth, and wronged the People
'call'd *Quakers*, both in Charge, Citation and,
'Ob-

'Observation in his said Sheet, &c. Thus far then we agreed as to Matter of Debate : I in my Sheet offer'd to produce every Book and Page quoted, before ten or twelve impartial Men : And *G. W.* offered to make it appear, before *any* six, ten, or twelve moderate Men, that I had wronged them : So that nothing remained now but my coming to *London* to joyn Issue with *G. W.* and pursuant the 27th of *January* 1693. I did, and sent him the Charge following ; which had he kept to his word [*any thing*] we had debated the matter ; but nothing would do with him but Quakers on his side, which tho' I was loth, yet upon condition of a retractation of what I proved against them, and which they could not justifie, I at last consented, and to that I held them, seeing it is, as above observed, their own method, proposed by *Edw. Burroughs* and *W. Penn*, to the *Papists.* And whether I have not herein acquitted myself, I leave the World to judge.

Francis Bugg's *Charge against the Quakers.*

1. THEY deny Jesus of *Nazareth*, who was born of the Blessed Virgin *Mary* to be Christ, and the efficient cause of Man's Salvation, &c.

2. Their Books are Blasphemous, and their Practices Idolatrous.

B 2　　　3. They

3. They deny the Scriptures, by fpeaking contemptuoufly of them, calling them Death, Duft, and Serpents-meat; and that Preaching out of them is Conjuration.

4. They defpife the Ordinances of Jefus Chrift, as Baptifm and the Lord's Supper, faying, They arofe from the Pope, and are no part of God's Worfhip; to which their practice of laying them afide as ufelefs fay *Amen.*

5. They undervalue the Death and Sufferings of our Lord Jefus Chrift.

6. They exalt their own Writings above the Scriptures, and their own Sufferings above the Sufferings of Chrift.

Obferve, that I do not charge thefe Errors upon all that go under the Name of *Quakers,* as *George Keith,* and divers others that are feparate from the *Foxonian* Party, who alfo charge them with Damnable Herefies and Doctrins of Devils, and fuch Errors as no *Proteftant Society* would tolerate, *&c.* as at large in their Book extant,*&c.* and as in *New-Rome unmask'd, &c.* I have more largely explained my felf, *p.* 68. to 71.

Francis Bugg's *particular Charge againft* George Whitehead.

1. **H**E is a publick Defamer. 2. A wicked Forger. 3. A wilful Lyer. 4. A grofs Perverter. 5. A falfe Gloffer. 6. A

de-

deceiver of the People. This I offer to prove, and when done, before the same Men to answer any Charge which G. *W.* shall exhibit against me,

Francis Bugg.

Here follows the substance of the Letter I sent him as Cover to the Charge.

In answer to your faint Challenge in your pretended Vindic. p. 4. *to meet me in any place in* London, *I am come to prove both the general and particular recited Charge before eight moderate Ministers, each of us to chuse four, excepting against* Quakers, Ranters, *and* Muggletonians, *but give you your choice, whether to chuse the whole number out of the* Episcopalians, Presbyterians, Independants, *or* Baptists; *or whether each of us one out of each: This I leave to you. And since you are of late for distinguishing the Moderate from the more Rigid, if your Case be good, I hope you cannot but think there is four Moderate Men amongst them all, who have both Reason and Sence to judge of Matter of Fact.*

Fr. Bugg.

This he refused, which shewed he either doubted his Case, or that he had such Incharity, as not to think there were four moderate, wise, and just Men in all the four Societies; if the last, what signifie his pretended distinguishing? If the first, why does he so bitterly complain, that I wrong them in

B 3 Charge,

Charge, Citation, and Obfervation ? But his word [*any*] gave me my choice ; fo when he refufed the Terms abovefaid, I made him a fecond Propofal, *viz.* to prove my Charge exhibited, alfo my Sheet to the Parliament, and if I have afferted any thing falfely, to retract it under my Hand, before fix Members of Parliament, each of us to chufe three, upon condition that you will do the fame. Sent and fubfcribed in the prefence of *Samuel Grove, Samuel Place, Henry Symons, John Fenn, Daniel Haffel,* by me

Fra. Bugg.

This he alfo refufed, either judging we could not find each of us three moderate Men in the Houfe of Commons, or elfe he went from his words, to leave it to *any* fix, ten, or twelve moderate Men of Common Sence and Honefty : Nay, that is not all, but he ftill refufes to abide by *Burrough*'s Propofition above recited : But that he might not have a ftartinghole, I fent him a third Offer, *viz.*

   ' *G. W.* I was minded to except againft
' *Quakers,* as in my firft and fecond Propofal
' I did, becaufe I know they cannot be im-
' partial between us ; but becaufe I perceive
' you cannot otherwife be prevailed withal, I
' will renew my Offer, *viz.* do you chufe
' three Men where you pleafe in the King's
' Dominion, and I will chufe three ; and I
' offer to prove my Charge on condition, that

' you

'you will engage under your Hand, that
'what the *Quakers* hold you will either juftifie
'by Scripture, or retract under your Hand, as
'alfo what your felf have wrote : And I do
'hereby engage the like, &c.

Fra. Bugg.

This he alfo refufed to abide by, upon the
account of a retractation ; tho' *Ed. B.* in the
name of the *Quakers*, offered not only to retract, but alfo to renounce all their Religion,
and to confefs to all the World under his
Hands, that they have been deceived, &c. as
at large in his Epiftle above-mentioned : But
ftill I purfued him, and fent him a fourth
Offer, *viz.*

Feb. 9th. 1693.

'G. W. yours receiv'd, and return you the
'Terms upon which I offered to debate the
'Controverfie, according to Agreement in
'other Circumftances ; I ask no more than I
'give, which is equal : I am not confcious to
'my felf of being guilty of what you either
'have or now do charge me with, and that
'encourages me to engage a retractation, if
'need be : If you think yourfelf clear of my
'Charge, and that the *Quakers* hold no fuch
'Errors as I lay to their charge, what make
'you fo timerous of engaging under your
'Hands to retract, if proved upon you ? If
'you think a retractation will marr the beau-
'ty of your pretence to write and fpeak by'

B 4

'and

' and from an Infallible Spirit, remember
' that *Hungate* the Jesuite, who profeſſed In-
' fallibility almoſt equal with the *Quakers*, did
' not refuſe to ſubſcribe when he diſputed
' with Biſhop *Bramhal.* Read the Life of the
' ſaid Biſhop. Beſide, you ſee *E. B.* allowed
' the point : Nay, moreover it was *W. Penn*'s
' way with the Papiſts ; ſee his *Seaſonable Ca-*
' *veat, &c. p.* 35. To conclude, (ſays *W. P.*)
' if we would not receive a Thief until he has
' repented, let the Papiſts firſt *recant* of their
' voluminous *Errors,* not known in Scripture,
' nor ever heard of for Three hundred years
' together after Chriſt, *&c.* Yet if you will
' leave the Matter to diſintereſted perſons, ac-
' cording to the latitude of your Offer in your
' printed Sheet, *viz. to* any *Moderate Men of*
' *Sence and Common Honeſty, &c.* I will require
' no retractation, but leave it to them, whe-
' ther I have wronged you in Charge, Cita-
' tion, or Obſervation. And as to the twelve
' Witneſſes, for whom you make ſuch a
' complaint, if upon examination I do not
' prove them guilty of Perjury, on your own
' Propoſitions to Authority, I will retract my
' Proceedings againſt them ; but if I do prove
' it, then you ſhall engage, that they ſhall re-
' tract under their Hands, always excepting
' againſt the ſaid twelve Falſe-witneſſes, being
' preſent at the Debate, unleſs it be when the
' four particulars in their Certificate be under
' examination ; or when any Matter depend-
' ing thereon be under conſideration.

Fra. Bugg.

But

But all would not do ; I could not get *Sheba*, the Son of *Bichri*, that Man of *Belial*, 2 *Sam.* 20. to come out on equal Terms : Neither will their People, like the wife Women in *Abel*, bring him out ; and thereupon I shall leave it to the World, whether I have not performed what I promised in my Sheet; and whether *G. W.* have not shuffled and evaded a fair Debate, 1*st*, in refusing to leave the Matter to *any* moderate Men, as he promised in print ; 2. And when debated before his Friends, who are Parties in the Errors, and cannot give it against him, refuse to subscribe a Retractation, according to the Offer of their great Prophet *Edw. Burroughs,* and *W. P.* But before I proceed to prove my Charge, I would premise some few things, *viz.*

Firft, *The Quakers Vind.* &c. *p.* 1. ' It's not ' unknown unto you (the Parliament) that ' we are Diffenters from the Church of *England,* and as *fuch* we enjoy our Liberty un- ' der you; and confequently we ought not ' to be reputed Criminal for being fuch, *&c.*

I grant, that barely for being fuch, you ought not to be reputed criminal : But if under that notion you take Liberty not only to maintain and defend fuch Errors, as tend to overthrow the Chriftian Faith, but alfo print, expofe and fpread your erronious Books all over *England* and *Wales,* and beyond the Seas, unlicens'd to the Scandal of Religion; and not content therewith neither, but to indict me for printing and expofing unlicens'd:

. This

This seems criminal, at least very bold : For if you would not be reputed *Criminal*, because your Opinion is for the present indulg'd, forgetting perhaps that you stand but upon your good Behaviour, why should you repute such as see your Errors, and forsake you, (and conform themselves to the Establish'd Religion, as that which is more true and orthodox) *Criminal*, calling me a *Self-condemn'd Apostate*? Is not this throwing Dirt in the Face of the Government, rendering their Religion so false and erroneous, as that whoever forsake, and conform to the Establish'd Religion, must therefore be *Self-condemn'd Apostates*? Do you think this may not affect your Superiors, so as to consider of your bold Adventures, *&c.*

Again, ' That *Fra. Bugg* himself did not ' account us Criminal for our Principles two ' years after he left us, and joyned himself to ' the Church of *England*, *&c.* For which he quotes my Book, *The Quakers detected, and their Errors confuted.*

To which I answer, The very Title shews the contrary : And in the Book I charge them with *False Doctrin, Erroneous Principles*; their *Teachers Cruel Taskmasters, Persecutors*, and *Tyrants*; and that part of their Doctrin, which was true, (as I still believe some little of what they teach is true) served only as *a Decoy to catch simple Souls by*; charging their Ministers with Lyes, gross Forgery, and scandalous Defamations, *Babel's* Builders, *Pharisaical* Hypocrites : See p. 4, 5, 18, 21. And now let the
Wife

Wife in Heart judge, whether I did not account the Quakers criminal in 1686. With what face then can this gross Perverter *G. W.* say I did not account them criminal in 1686. unless to be guilty of the forementioned be not criminal ? As by the Quakers persisting therein, they should not account it : However I did then, and do now, account them great Criminals, both in Doctrin and Practice, and for leaving them am not condemned ; but bless the Day that ever I forsook such an Heresie as I deem them to hold, defend, and I fear wilfully maintain.

The Matters in that Book treated on I methodiz'd under these three general Heads, *viz.* The first point under Consideration was, *How I came to be a Member of their Society :* The second, *How I came to see their Errors and leave them :* The third, *How I came perswaded and satisfied in going to the Publick.* In the first I did set forth what I thought of them in 58, and 60. and what they preached, and how innocent they appeared : *G. W.* in *Norwich-*Castle seemed as demure as the best ; yet in that Book I set forth, as I then believed that all was but a *Decoy* or *Cheat*, to draw *Disciples* after them ; and if I was cheated and mistaken in them, so was *Hugh Latimore*, that learned Prelate, in the smooth Carriage of the Papists, and their Infallible Delusions, who said, ' I am ignorant of things which I trust hereaf-' ter to know, *&c.* Read *Fox's Acts and Monuments, &c. p.* 410, 467, 468, 1325, 1488.
where

where Bifhop *Latimer,* Bifhop *Cranmer,* M. *Luther,* Dr. *Barns,* and other pious fincere Chriftians, have not been too good nor too holy to acknowledge themfelves miftaken, upon conviction, though by your Doctrin render'd Apoftates, in that they once thought the *Popifh* Doctrine true, *&c.* Nay, your Incharity renders many of your own People Apoftates, who before they were deluded by your black Art of calling the Scripture *Death, Duft,* and *Serpents-meat,* the Ordinances *an Inftitution of the Whore of Rome,* the publick Minifters *Witches, Devils, Gormandizing Priefts,* &c. thought the Doctrine of the Church of *England* found and orthodox : But fince they are turn'd to the Herefie of Quakerifm, *G. W.* accounts them Saints, Lambs, Prophets, and what not ? But as thefe Weights are counterfeit, fo I purpofe to try them by the Touchftone of the Scripture, which cannot lye. And I refer to my Book, *New-Rome unmask'd,* &c. containing more than 100 Pages in Quarto, divided into twelve Chapters, which fhew at large, that forfaking the Quakers is no Apoftacy from the Articles of the Chriftian Faith, *&c.* fold by Mr. *Dunton* at the *Raven* in the *Poultry,* and Mr. *Guillam* Bookfeller in *Bifhopfgate-Street.* Concluding my Introduction with St. *Auguftine, Errare poffum hæreticus effe non poffum.*

The

The FIRST CHARGE
Against the
Quakers,

That they Deny Jesus of Nazareth, *who was born of the Blessed Virgin* Mary, *to be* Christ, *and the Efficient Cause of Man's Salvation.*

The ARGUMENT.

THE Method proposed to prove the recited Charge, is, 1*st*. A brief Citation of Scriptures proving, that Jesus is the Christ of God, and Efficient Cause of Man's Salvation, from the Testimony of G O D, Angels, and Men. 2*dly*. A Recital out of the *Quakers* Books, wrote by their most approved Authors, alledging the contrary, shewing them thereby to be of a different Faith from the Prophets, Apostles, Saints, and Blessed Martyrs, and all true Christians to this day. 3*dly*. That *Geo. Fox*, the first Founder of *Quakerism, Anno* 1650. have since assumed to himself those divine Attributes due only to Christ, and thereby hath overthrown the
Faith

Faith of some. *4thly.* That his Disciples and Followers, and such of greatest note amongst them, hath said *Amen* to his Blasphemies, by their frequent Adorations of him, as the *Star,* the *Branch,* the *Son of Righteousness, &c.*

1st. Scripture Texts proving *Jesus* to be *Christ.*

John 1. 14. *And the word was made flesh, and dwelt amongst us : (and we beheld his glory, the glory as of the only begotten of the Father) full of grace and truth.* Luke 1. 26. *And in the sixth month the Angel* Gabriel *was sent from* God *unto a city of* Gallilee, *named* Nazareth : *and the Angel said unto her, Fear not* Mary, *for thou hast found favour with* God : *and behold, thou shalt conceive in thy womb, and bring forth a son, and shalt call his name* Jesus. 2. 10, 11. *And the Angel said unto them, Fear not* ; *for behold, I bring unto you good tydings of great joy, which shall be unto all people* ; *for unto you is born this day, in the city of* David, *a Saviour, Christ the* Lord. Mark 9.7. Matt. 17.5. *While he yet spake, behold a bright cloud overshadowed them : and behold a voice out of the cloud, which said, This is my beloved son, in whom I am well pleased, hear him.* Matt. 26. 67. *Then did they spit in* his face, *and buffeted* him, *and others smote* him *with the palms of their hands.* 27. 38. *Then there were two thieves crucified with him, one on the right hand, another on the left. Ver.* 50. *Jesus, when he had cried again with a loud voice, yielded up the ghost.* 28. 6: He
is

is not here, for he is riſen, *as he ſaid, Come ſee the place where the Lord lay.* Acts 1. 9, 10, 11. *While they beheld,* he *was taken up, and a cloud* received him *out of their ſight. And while they looked ſtedfaſtly towards Heaven, as he went up, behold two men ſtanding by them in white apparel, which alſo ſaid, Ye men of* Gallilee, *why ſtand ye gazing up into Heaven ?* This ſame Jeſus *which is taken up from you into Heaven* [then not in them, in the *Quakers* ſence ; for as he ſaid with reference to his Perſon, *Matt.* 26. 11. *Me ye have not always*] *ſhall ſo come in like manner as ye have ſeen him go into Heaven.* Acts 5. 30, 31. *The God of our fathers raiſed up* Jeſus, *whom ye* ſlew, *and* hanged *on a* Tree, him *hath God exalted with his right hand, to be a* Prince *and a* Saviour, *for to give repentance to* Iſrael, *and forgiveneſs of ſins.* Acts 2. 36. *Therefore let all the houſe of* Iſrael *know aſſuredly, that God hath made the ſame* Jeſus, *whom ye have crucified, both Lord and Chriſt.* Heb. 5. 9. *And being made perfect, he became the Author of eternal ſalvation to all them that obey him.* 12. 2. *Looking unto* ⸲*Jeſus the author and finiſher of our faith, who for the joy that was ſet before him endured the croſs, deſpiſing the ſhame, and is ſet down at the right hand of the throne of God.* Rom. 8. 34. *It is Chriſt that died, yea rather, that is riſen again, who is at the right hand of God, who alſo maketh interceſſion for us.* Acts 7. 35. *But he being full of the Holy Ghoſt, looked up ſtedfaſtly into Heaven, and ſaw the glory of God and* Jeſus *ſtanding on the right hand of God.* Ver. 56. *And ſaid, Behold,*

I ſee

I see the Heavens opened, and the son of man stan-
ding on the right hand of God. Acts 10. 38. to 44.
How God anointed Jesus *of* Nazareth *with the*
Holy Ghost, and with power, who went about doing
good ——*And we are witnesses of all things which*
he did both in the land of the Jews *and in* Jerusa-
lem. *Whom* ye slew *and hanged on a* tree, him
God raised up the third day, and shewed him open-
ly, Not to all the people, but to witnesses chosen be-
fore of God, even to us, who did eat and drink
with him after he rose *from the dead. And he*
commanded us to preach unto the people, and to
testifie, that it is he *which was ordained of God to*
be judge of the quick and dead. To him give all
the Prophets witness, that through his *name who-*
soever believeth in him, shall receive remission
of sins. Read 1 Cor. 15. 15.

2dly. *The* Quakers *teach the contrary.*

A Question to Professors, p. 33. 'Now the
' Scriptures do expresly distinguish between
' Christ and the Garment which he wore;
' between *him* that came, and the *body* in
' which *he* came; between the Substance
' which was veiled, and the Veil which vei-
' led it. *Lo, I come, a body hast thou prepared me.*
' There was plainly he, and the Body in which
' *he* came; there was the outward Vessel, and
' the inward Life: This we certainly know,
' and can never call the Bodily Garment
' *Christ,* but that which appeared and dwelt
' in the Body.

Ob-

Obſerve how flatly they contradict the holy Scripture Teſtimony, and how they would divide the Humanity from the Godhead; which is, in plain terms, a plain denyal of Chriſt; for if they can never call him that was born of the Virgin *Mary* Chriſt, whom the Jews ſpit upon, ſmote with the palms of their Hands, nailed to the Croſs, hanged on a Tree, and at laſt crucified him; I ſay, if they can *never* call him *Chriſt,* but *a Veil, a Garment, a Figure, &c.* they can never own him to be Chriſt, and conſequently deny him to be Chriſt; and not only ſo, but acquit the Jews, and their drudge *Judas* of the Sin of murthering the Lord of Life and Glory; for when they laid hold of him, ſmote him, buffeted him, crowned him with Thorns, ſcourged him, nailed his tender Hands and Feet to the Croſs, pierced his Side, out of which came Water and Blood; they all this while, by the *Quaker's Doctrine,* did not lay hold upon nor touch Chriſt, and conſequently ought not to be charged with crucifying the Lord of Life and Glory; only, it's true, they took hold of a *Garment,* a *Veil, &c.* which they can *never* call *Chriſt.* Thus have they made the Apoſtles Falſe Witneſſes, acquitted *Judas,* and clear'd the hard hearted unbelieving Jews of all their Barbarities inhumanly inflicted on the Bleſſed Jeſus.

A Queſt. &c. *p.* 27. ' Is not the Subſtance, ' the Life, called *Chriſt,* where-ever it is ' found ? Doth not the Name [*Chriſt*] be-

C   ' long

' long to the whole Body, and to every Mem-
' ber in the Body, as well as to the Head *&c?*

Obferve how *Matt.* 24. 24. is fulfilled by
their Doctrine ; every believing *Quaker* may
be called Chrift as well as he that fuffered
Death upon the Crofs · Oh, dreadful Blafphemy! And to confirm it, he tells you
about ten lines after, *viz. That the Name is
not given to the Veffel,* &c. O Impudence
itfelf! did not the Angel fay, That *unto you
is born this day, in the city of* David, *a Saviour,
which is* Chrift the Lord ? *Luke* 2. 11. & *v.*28.
Simon *took him in his arms, and bleffed God, and
faid, Lord, now letteft thou thy fervant depart
in peace, according to thy word ; for mine eyes
have feen thy falvation,* &c. So that to fay the
Name *Chrift* belongs to every Believer, as well
as to him, is Blafphemy ; for the Apoftle to
the *Coloffians* gives the Name not only to the
Godhead in him, but to him in whom it
dwelt, which they contemptuoufly term the
Garment, *Col.* 2. 9.

The Chriftian Quaker, and his Divine Teft,&c.
part 1. *p.* 107. ' To conclude, *We,* though this
' general Victory was obtained, and holy Pri-
' vileges therewith, and that the Holy Body
' was not inftrumentally without a fhare
' thereof; yet that the efficient and chiefeft
' caufe was the Light and Life.— *P.* 111. So
' that thus far we can approach the honefter
' fort of Profeffors of Religion, *&c.*

Ob-

Obferve how far the Quaker's Approach to the Chriftians amount to: The Chriftians believe, that he who was born of the Virgin *Mary*, who was fpit upon, buffeted, fmote with the palms of their Hands, dyed, rofe again, and afcended into *Heaven*, in the fight of the *Gallileans*, and now fits at the right hand of God, according to the recited Scriptures; I fay, they believe the fame Jefus to be the Chrift of God ; and that he is both the effi. cient and chief caufe of Man's Salvation: *Aɛ̃s* 4. 10, 12. *By the name of Jefus of* Nazareth, *whom ye have crucified, whom God raifed from the dead, even by him doth this man ftand here before you whole. Neither is there falvation in any other, for there is none other name given under Heaven among men, whereby we muft be faved,* &c.   So that the Profeffor's Faith and Hopes of Salvation are in the crucified Jefus, which you call the Holy Body.   Indeed, you do approach to them a little, in calling his Body *Holy*, and allowing him to have fome fhare in the Salvation of Mankind *inftrumentally* ; but the chief and efficient caufe is in the light which you have in your felves, and which was in the Jews and Gentiles before. the Incarnation of our Bleffed Lord and Saviour ; which if that had been fufficient, what need was there for Chrift's coming, fince he is but inftrumentally a Saviour ? For fo you allow good Men to be, as I fhall fhew anon : So that your Approach to the Chriftians is very fmall, even but a few fteps; for

the

the unbelieving Jews thought him to be a good Man, *viz. Elias, Jeremias,* or one of the old Prophets ; but inftead of preffing on, the Author turns himfelf round to his old Friends the *Quakers,* and tell them his Meaning by this fudden and unufual Approach.

P. 102. ' So that the Invifible Life was the
' Root and Fountain of all, which is fome-
' times afcribed in Scripture to the Body, by
' that common figure or way of fpeaking
' amongft Men, the thing containing which,
' is the *Body* for the thing contained, which
was the Life, *&c.*

Obferve, I always underftood, that when we call a Houfe that is made of Lime and Stone a *Church,* that it was a figurative way of fpeaking the thing containing for the thing contained ; but I never knew this diftinction touching our Bleffed Saviour made by any others than the *Quakers ;* and their chief Reafon is, That they having the fame Light, Life and Spirit in their Bodies, as was in his Body, they would have every Man a Saviour, every Man a Chrift : For, as above, they fay, *The Name of Chrift belongs to every Member of the Body, as well as the Head :* And where ever they make an Approach to the true Profeffors of Chriftianity, 'tis only for a Decoy : For as above obferved, they can *never* call the Bodily Garment *Chrift,* meaning him that was born of the Virgin, but *a Garment, a Veil, a Figure,* an *inftrumental Caufe* of *Salvation,* but not the *efficient ;* the thing containing for

ano.

another, *viz.* for the thing contained : For to call him that was born of the Virgin, who suffered Death on the Cross, Died, Rose again, and ascended; this is but a metaphorical Speech, the thing containing for the thing contained. Thus have they robbed the Blessed Jesus of one of his emanent Attributes, *viz.* of being the efficient Cause of Man's Salvation. Thus do they dance the Rounds, sometimes approaching to the Christian Professors; as if they were in good earnest : but by and by, with a sudden turn they glide to their Brethren, and insinuate by consequence, That him that was born of the Virgin, he is no otherwise a Saviour [let the Episcopalians, Presbiterians, Independents and Baptists say what they will to the contrary] than other good Men are, *&c.*

P. 102, 103. ‘ I dare not attribute to an *Ex-*
‘ *ternal* prepared Being,(*That*)which is the na-
‘ tural and proper Work of the Divine Light :
‘ But certainly, if some Men in Scripture
‘ are entituled *Saviours*, because of their
‘ Contribution, of their Trials, Travels and
‘ Labours towards the Salvation of Mankind ;
‘ of much more right is that Honour ascri-
‘ bed to him, who had the Spirit without
‘ measure, *&c.*

Observe, the best Approach I take notice of, is, That they do seemingly allow him to have the Spirit without measure ; but I cannot call it otherwise than *seeming*, since 'tis but about eight Lines after, where speaking of

Salva-

Salvation, he fays, *And to the Holy Manhood not any otherwise than Inftrumentally* ; which in the Paragraph above recited, he there allows to good and holy Men, and that as a meritorious Reward too, *viz.* Becaufe of the Contribution of their Trials, Travels, and Labours towards the Salvation of Mankind. So that by the Quakers Doctrine, good Men are Inftrumentally Saviours : And Chrift himfelf is no more but Inftrumentally a Saviour. The Firft I grant, as they are Servants to Chrift, and by his hand of Providence made ufe of towards the Converfion of others. The Laft I deny, as an Heretical Doctrine, which tends to rob Chrift of one of his chiefeft Jewels; as the next Paffage will demonftrate.

P 129. ' That neverthelefs not to the Body, but Holy Light of Life therein is chief-'ly to be afcribed the Salvation ; and to the 'Body, however excellent, but Inftrumen-'tally.'

Obferve, how with one Shoulder they bear down the Bleffed Jefus, as only a Body, inftrumentally ferviceable, contrary to the Teftimony of St. *Luke,* and the infpired Apoftles and Holy Prophets, who foretold of the coming of the Juft one. And fince 'tis a great and precious Priviledge, that we have the Holy Scriptures in a known Tongue, that thereby we may have recourfe thereunto, to rectifie our Miftakes, and help our Judgments, and prove the Articles of our Chriftian Faith : So am I willing to prove my

Charge

Charge against the Quakers from plain matter of Fact, out of their own Books, writ by
the most Learned amongst them; and by
the Coherence of their Doctrine, confuted
by Scripture, Reason, and Authority, shall
this Controversie be decided. For if the
good Deed of the Woman, *Matth.* 26. 13.
done to Christ against his Burials shall be told
of her so long as the Gospel is preached, surely so long as the Gospel is preached shall
there be War made against such false Teachers, as shall thus bring in damnable Heresies,
denying the Lord Jesus Christ to be a Compleat Saviour, *&c.* But once more pray hear
him.

   P. 97, 98. ' The Serpent is a Spirit: Now
' no thing can bruise the Head of the Serpent,
' but something that is Spiritual, as the Ser-
' pent is. But if that Body of Christ were
' the Seed, then could he not bruise the Ser-
' pents Head in all, because the Body of
' Christ is not so much as in any one; and
' consequently, the Seed of the Promise is an
' Holy Principle of Light and Life, that be-
' ing received into the Heart, bruiseth the
' Serpents Head. And because the *Seed*
' *which cannot be that Body* is Christ, as testifie
' the Scriptures, the Seed is one, and that Seed
' is Christ, *&c.*

   And thus have I traced him in his divers
Turnings and manifold Approaches; sometimes to the Professors, and back again to
the Quakers, until at last you see he denies
the

the Body which was born of the Virgin,
to be Chrift: And the reafon he gives, is,
Becaufe he is not perfonally in every Man,
and fo no way capable to conquer the Serpent in them ; and therefore not the Chrift :
But if they were humble, and would forfake
their Errours , and by Faith lay hold. of
Chrift, who is the Seed of the Promife, *Gen.*
3. 14. confeffing their Sins, and begging Pardon for Chrift's fake, let them not doubt but
the Head of the Serpent in them fhall be
bruifed. But if they thus contemn the Bleffed
Jefus, who was born of the Virgin, &c. one
calling him a Garment, which they can never call Chrift ; another, becaufe he is not
perfonally in every Man,he cannot be Chrift ;
and by and by the Name *Chrift* belongs to
every Member, as well as to the Head ; for
that they have Light, Life and Spirit in them,
as Chrift had : another, that Chrift is not a
Compleat Saviour, otherwife than inftrumentally ; nor no otherwife to be called Chrift,
than metaphorically, or by that common
Figure or way of fpeaking, *viz.* the thing
containing for the thing contained : I fay,
fo long as they continue in their Unbelief, its
no marvel they complain fo much of the Serpent's having Dominion in them.

The Sandy Foundation fhaken,&c. P.21. 'The
'Juftice offended being Infinite, his Satisfa-
'ction ought to bear a Proportion therewith,
'which Jefus Chrift as Man could never pay,
'*he being Finite* ; and from a *Finite* Caufe
could

' could never proceed an Infinite Effect : For
' *so* Man may be said to bring forth God,
' since no thing below the Divinity it self
' can righly be styled Infinite.

I have much more to say against the dangerous Errors in that Book , which came lately to my hand ; but I spare the Author. However, by what is said, 'tis plain that they account him that was born of the Virgin but a Man, a Finite Creature, a Vail, a Garment, a Saviour instrumentally like other good Men , and which they cannot call Christ. Nay further, they say he is not Christ, not being personally in every Man : And the Consequence is both natural and plain, that they deny Jesus of *Nazareth.*

Smith's Primer, P. 8. How may I know when Christ is truly Preached ?

Answ. They that are false (Ministers) preach Christ without, and bid People believe in him as he is in Heaven above ; but they that are Christ's Ministers, preach Christ within.

Smith's Catechism, P. 57. *And is that which is within you the only Foundation upon which you stand, and the Principle of your Religion?*

Answ. *That of God within us is so, for we know it is Christ; and being Christ, it must needs be* only *and* principal; *for that which is* only, *admits not of another; and that which is* principal, *is greatest in being : And thus we know Christ in us to be unto us the* only *and* principal, &c.

The Sword of the Lord drawn, &c. P. 5. Your
‘ imagined God beyond the Stars, and your
‘ carnal Chrift is utterly denied.——That this
‘ Chrift is God and Man in one Perfon is a
‘ Lie.

By which, without enlarging, ’tis very
plain, That as they do not own Jefus of *Nazareth,* who was born of the Virgin, Suffered,
Died, Rofe, and Afcended, and now fits at
the Right Hand of God in Heaven above;
fo all that preach the fame Chrift, and bid
People believe in him as he is in Heaven
above, are, by the Quakers Doctrine, Falfe
Minifters : But they that preach the Light
within, as the only Foundation which admits of no other, and as the principal Cor-
ner-ftone of their Building. Thefe, and thefe
only are (fay they) true Minifters. And this,
if nothing had been faid before, had been fufficient to prove my firft Charge; namely,
That the Quakers deny Jefus of *Nazareth,*
who was born of the Bleffed Virgin, to be
Chrift, and the Efficient Caufe of Man’s
Salvation : And I pray God to give them a
Heart to repent them of their Unbelief.

1. *By* Geo. Fox’s *affuming Divine Attri-*
butes to himfelf.

News caming up out of the North, &c. P. 1.
‘ Written from the Mouth of the Lord : From
‘ one who is naked, and ftands naked before
‘ the Lord : Cloathed with Righteoufnefs,
whofe

whoſe Name is not *known* in the World, riſen up out of the North, which was propheſied of, but now it is fulfilled, *&c.* G. F.

The Teachers of the World unvailed, &c. P.26. I am the Light ; him by whom the World was made ; and doth enlighten every Man that comes into the World : If you love the Light which you are enlightned with-'all, you will love Chriſt, who ſaith, *Learn of me :* But if you hate that Light, there is your Condemnation from him, who is * one with the Truth in every Man, who of the Lord was moved this to write, that People might ſee what hath gotten up ſince the Apoſtles time out of the Light, with the Light, and reigned out of the Light, but now is manifeſt with the Light, which the Apoſtles were in, it is ſeen, and to the Children of Light now is manifeſt, whoſe Name of the World is called G. F.

> * Here Is a Fourth Perſon added to the Trinity, accor-ding to their Do-ctrine.

Several Petitions Anſwered, &c. P. 60. ' My ' Name is covered from the World ; and the ' World knows *not me, nor my Name.* —He ' that overcometh, hath the new Name, and ' knoweth it. ——He that overcometh, ſit-' teth in his Throne: He that overcometh is ' Crowned : ——He that overcometh, eateth ' of the Hidden Manna : He that overco-' meth ſhall inherit all things. ——He that ' hath an Ear to hear let him hear ; and blessed

' bleſſed is he that reads, and doth underſtand
' what he reads.   G. F.

Saul'*s Errand to* Damaſcus, *p.* 7. ' The Old
' Man cannot endure to hear the New Man
' ſpeak, which is Chriſt, and Chriſt is the
' Way ; and if Chriſt be in you, muſt not he
' ſay, *I am the Way, the Truth, and the Life ?*
' *P.* 8. ' And he that hath the ſame Spirit
' that raiſed up Jeſus Chriſt from the Dead is
' equal with God.   G. F.

The Second Charge againſt the Quakers.

Their Books are blaſphemous, and their Pra-
   ctite Idolatrous, &c. *which is proved in*
   the foregoing and following, to the confu-
   tation of G. W. *and his falſe Witneſſes,*
   who deny theſe Appellations, &c.

This is only to go amongſt Friends.

' THou, O North of *England !* who art
' counted as deſolate and barren, and
' reckoned the leaſt of the Nations, yet out
' of thee did the *Branch* ſpring and *Star* ariſe,
' which gives light to all the Regions round
' about ; in thee the Son of Righteouſneſs
                                      ' ap-

appeared with Wounding and with Healing, &c.

The next is *John Blackling*'s Certificate, see Part V. *Christ. Quak. distinguish'd, &c. p.* 77. ' That G. *Fox* is blessed with Honour above ' many Brethren ; and, That Thousands will ' stand by him in a Heavenly Record ; ' —— That his Life reigns, and is spotless, ' innocent, and still retains his Integrity, ' whose Eternal Honour and Blessed Renown ' shall remain ; yea, his presence, and the ' dropping of his tender words in the Lord's ' Love, was my Soul's Nourishment.

The Quaker's Challenge, p. 6. of G. *Fox* thus in brief : ' A Prophet indeed. —— It was ' said of Christ, *he was in the World, and the* ' *World was made by him, and the World knew* ' *him not* : *So* it may be said of this true Pro- ' phet, whom *John* said he was not ; but thou ' shalt feel this Prophet one day as heavy as ' a Milstone upon thee ; and though the ' World knew him not, yet he is known.

Sol. Eccles.

Jos. Coale's *Letter to* G. Fox, *out of the* Barbadoes, *thus in brief:*

' DEar G.*Fox*, who art the Father of many ' Nations, whose Life has reached thro' ' us thy Children, even to the Isles afar off, ' to the begetting many again to a lively ' hope, for which Generations to come shall ' call thee blessed, whose Being and Habita- ' tion

' tion is in the power of the Higheſt, in which,
' thou rules and governs in Righteouſneſs,
' and thy Kingdom is eſtabliſhed in Peace,
' and the Encreaſe thereof is without end.

Joſ. Coale.

Another from John Audland *to* G. F. *out of the
Weſt of* England.

' DEar and precious one, in whom my
' Life is bound up, and my Strength in
' thee ſtands ; by thy Breathings I am nou-
' riſhed ; by thee my Strength is renewed ;
' Bleſſed art thou for evermore, and bleſſed
' are all that enjoy thee : Life and Strength
' comes from thee holy one ; — daily do I
' find thy preſence with me, which doth ex-
' ceedingly preſerve me, for I cannot reign,
' but in thy preſence and power ; pray for
' me, that I may ſtand in thy Dread for ever-
' more. ——— I am thine begotten, and nou-
' riſhed by thee; and in thy Power am I
' preſerved : Glory unto thee, Holy One, for
' ever.   *John Audland.*

*Brief Obſervations upon the Two laſt
Particulars.*

1. G. *Fox*'s aſſuming Divine Attributes to
himſelf, *viz. Firſt*, He tells you, he wrote from
the Mouth of God himſelf, ſtands naked, clo-
thed only with Righteouſneſs; which was
propheſied and fulfilled. *Secondly*, That he
is

is the light of the World, by whom it was
made *One*, with the Truth in every Man.
Thirdly, That he was so covered, as that nei-
ther himself nor his Name was known in the
World, had a new Name, plac'd in his
Throne, was Crowned, inherited all things,
Christ in him might say, *I am the way, the
truth, and the life,* alluding to *John* 14. 6. And
Fourthly, He that had the same Spirit which
raised Jesus, was equal with God : Which
Spirit he pretended to have.

2. How *Fox* s Disciples ecchoed back Adorations, which answered as Face answers Face
in a Glass ; for he could not magnifie himself, but his Proselytes were ready to cry *Ho-
sanna : First,* Oh thou North of *England*, de-
solate the least of the Nations barren,*&c.* yet
out of thee did the Branch spring, the Star
arise, the Son of Righteousness appear, *&c.*
Alluding to *Micah* 5. 2. *Numb.* 24. 17. *Mal.*
4. 2. *Zech* 3. 8. And *Secondly,* That his Life
reigned and was spotless, his eternal Honour,
and blessed Renown,*&c.* *Thirdly,* A Prophet
indeed compared to Christ, as not known in
the World, though made by him. *Fourthly,*
Precious *George*, the Father of Nations, whose
Kingdom is established in Peace,the Encrease
thereof without end:Alluding to *Isa.*9.6,7. And
Fifthly, That they received Life and Strength
from him, preserved by him, could not reign
but in his power, begotten and nourished by
him, *&c.* Upon the whole matter, as there
were never greater Blasphemies spake by Man
than

than by *Fox,* fo never greater Adorations given to fuch a Sect-maſter. And yet *G. W.*
and *W. P.* in their Book *Judas and the Jews,*
p. 44. *Serious Search, &c.* p. 58. *Judgment Fixed, &c.* p. 19, 26. *Innocency againſt Envy, &c.*
p. 18. have Juſtified or Excuſed every Paſſage, except *John Audland's* Letter, which when
charged therewith by the *Athenian Mercury,*
June 11. 1692. *G.W.* did deny it to be of *J.A's*
writing. But we have the Original Letter,
and able to make it appear by comparing
Hands, to be his: Nor did *G. F.* deny it in his
Life-time, albeit an Abſtract thereof was Printed and Reprinted, *&c.*

The Third Charge againſt the
𝔔uakers.

That they deny the Scriptures, by ſpeaking
contemptuouſly of them : calling them,
Death, Duſt, Serpent's Meat, &c. and
that to Preach out of them is Conjura-
tion.

The ARGUMENT.

THis is one of their Errors I charged on
the *Quakers* in my Book, *New Rome un-
maſk'd,* &c. *Epiſt. Cr.* 6. and p. 78. This *G.W.*
procured Twelve Witneſſes, to teſtifie in the
Holy Fear of God, and on the behalf of
the

the Quakers, That they never fo believed, fo faid, nor fo affirmed: Which was fuch a notorious Lye ; and calling God to Record, I took it to amount to an Oath on their own Propofals to Authority: And not knowing a better way to manifeft them, I erected a Mock-Pillory, and Tried them, and found them guilty on their own Premifes. But the main matter now before me is, To prove the Truth in that particular, both in the cited Book *New Rôme*, &c. and the Sheet delivered to the Parliament : And in order to it I fhall firft recite their contemptuous Expreffions of the Holy Scripture ; and then confute their Arguments, which they bring to falve their Errour. And laftly fhew, That they extol their own Writings above the Scriptures, *viz.*

Their Contempt of the Holy Scriptures.

News coming up out of the North, &c. *p.* 14.
‘ And your Original is Carnal, Hebrew ,
‘ Greek; and Latin ; and your Word is Car-
‘ nal, the Letter ; and the Light is Carnal,
‘ the Letter ; and your Baptifm is Carnal.
‘ ——And their Communion is Carnal, a lit-
‘ tle Bread and Wine. —So duft is the Ser-
‘ pents Meat ; their Original is but Duft,
‘ which is but the Letter, which is Death.
‘ ——So the Serpent feeds upon Duft. —And
‘ their Gofpel is Duft, *Matthew, Mark, Luke,*
‘ and *John,* which is the Letter, *&c.*

D   Saul's

Saul's *Errand to* Damafcus, *&c.* p. 7. 'All
'that do ftudy to raife a Living thing out of
'a Dead, to raife the Spirit out of the Letter,
'are Conjurers, and draw Points and Rea-
'fons. ——They are Conjurers and Divi-
'ners, and their Teaching is from Conjura-
'tion, which is not fpoken from the Mouth
'of the Lord. ——The Letter of the Scrip-
'ture is carnal, and killeth, *&c.* G. F.

. David's *Enemies* difcovered, *&c.* p.7. 'And
'thefe (*i. e. Quakers*) do not call the Letter
'the Rule; and the Four Books, *Matthew*,
'*Mark*, *Luke* and *John*, the New Teftament
'or Gofpel, as thou, (*i. e.* the Publick Mi-
'nifter) and thy Generation do, thy Mini-
'ftry is in the Letter, which killeth.

G. *Whitehead* and *Ch. A.*
Truth's Defence, &c. p. 2. 104. 'You might
'as well have condemned the Scriptures to
'the Fire, as our Books and Papers: For our
'giving forth Papers and Printed Books, it is
'from the immediate, eternal Spirit of God.

Burrough's *Works*, &c. p. 51. 'And herein
'you have been bewitched from the Obedi-
'ence of the Truth within, to obey the Let-
'ter without. P. 47. That is no Command
'from God to me, what he commands to an-
'other : Neither did any of the Saints which
'we read of in Scripture, act by the Com-
'mand which was to another, not having the
'Command to themfelves.

The Quakers Refuge fixed upon, &c. p. 17.
'Whether the firft Pen-man of the Scrip-
'tures

'tures was *Moses* or *Hermes*; or whether
'both these, or not one; or whether there
'are not many Words contained in the Scrip-
'tures, which were not spoken by the Inspi-
'ration of the Holy Spirit: Whether some
'Words were not spoken by the Grand Im-
'postor; some by wicked Men; some by
'wise Men ill applied; some by good Men
'ill expressed; some by False Prophets, and
'yet true; some by True Prophets, and yet
'false, &c.

Several Petitions answered, &c. *p.* 30. 'And
'whereas we are moved to write abroad,
'shewing forth your Errors, that if ever you
'own the Prophets, Christ, and the Apostles
'(Writings,) ye will own them which are
'given forth by the same Power and Spirit,
'&c.

A Brief Discovery of a three fold Estate, &c.
p. 7. 'The Priests of the World are Conju-
'rers, raising dead Doctrines, dead Reasons,
'dead Uses, dead Motives, dead Tryals out
'of the Letter, which is Death; raising
'Death out of Death. Notable Conjurers!
'*P.* 9. *Babylon's* Merchants, selling Beastly
'Wares. ——The Letter, which is Dust
'and Death.

Observations thereupon.

1*st*, Observe, that they call the Holy Scripture Death, Dust, and Serpents-meat: If they
object, they mean the Letter abstractly from
the

the Spirit, that's but one of G. *W*'s Juggles ;
fee their Paper again ft *J. P. Aug.* 10. 1670.
viz. ' Whereas *J. P.* did bring to the Ex-
' change feveral Books and Writings, and
' amongft others the *Holy Scriptures, &c.*
Surely he could not burn the Holy Spirit
that gave them forth, as they molt wickedly
fuggefted he would have burnt the Bible. It
feems they can call the Bible *the Holy Scriptures* when for a wicked defign, and Duft,
and Death, and Serpents Meat, when they
fpeak their Judgment clearly. *2dly,* That
they are Conjurers that preach out of them :
Surely when they preach out of them, they
do not preach the Letter abftractly from the
Holy Doctrine and Bleffed Precepts therein
contained, but fome part of thofe holy Truths
therein contained ; and yet this preaching is,
by their Doctrine Conjuration and Witch-
craft, *&c. 3dly,* You may perceive that
G. *W.* and the *Quakers* do not call the four
Books of *Matthew, Mark, Luke,* and *John,*
either the New Teftament of Jefus Chrift, or
the Gofpel ; and why ? His Brother *Fox* fays
'tis Duft, Death, and Serpents-Meat : Yet to
ferve another turn, *Ellwood* writing again ft
W. R. in his Antidote, *p.* 81, 82. calls the Writings of the Evangelifts, *The New Teftament,
Scriptures of Truth, &c.* Oh the Deceit and
Self-contradiction of thefe *Babel*-Builders.
4tbly, You may fee they bring their own
Nonfence in competition with the holy Scripture and New Teftament : Nay, I fhall
                                        prove

prove by their Practice, that they prefer their own Pamphlets before the Scripture, and that beyond all their Glosses to the contrary. 5thly, That such as obey the Scriptures are bewitched from the Truth: And therefore, say they, That is no Command from God to me, what he commanded the Saints of old, recorded in Scripture; for, alas! what is the Scripture but a little Dust, Death, carnal Letter, Husk, Beastly Ware; and they that preach out of it Conjurers, notable Conjurers, *Babylon's* Merchants, yea, Witches, Devils, Gormandizing Priests, &c? 6thly, They insinuate by way of Query, That 'tis doubtful whether *Moses* or *Hermes* was the first Pen-man of *Holy Writ*; or whether either or neither; and so confound the Scriptures, as to overthrow its Divine Authority, suggesting that what is true the False-Prophets wrote, and what is false the True-Prophets wrote, and what is ill expressed and ill applied Wise and Good Men wrote, and by a Natural Invertion all the rest by Wicked Men, and the Grand Impostor. And I think they, by this time, have made room for the Atheists and Papists. This, I must confess, is such a cunning Stratagem of Satan and his Instruments, as the boldest Jesuit that ever I read of never attempted the like. And for more of it, I refer to *New* Rome *unmask'd*, &c. *p.* 23. And by this time I hope *G. W*'s Witnesses are convicted sufficiently, and for time to come will not say, the *Quakers* never

said,

said, affirmed, or believed, that the holy
Scriptures are Death, Duft, and Serpents-
Meat, *&c.*

But notwithftanding all this, and much
more that might be quoted of this nature,
yet *G. W.* boldly impofes upon the World,
that though they call·the Scripture Duft,
Death, and Serpents-meat, yet they do not
call the holy Scripture fo ; fee their pretended *Vindication, &c. p.* 2. *Effay, &c. p.* 5, 8.
but fay, *The holy Precepts and Doctrines they own :*
And from thence they'r called, fays *G.W.* holy
Scriptures. I grant it is for that very reafon that
the Chriftians call them *Holy Scriptures.* But on
the other hand I do pofitively affirm, That it
is for · that very Reafon that the *Quakers* call
them Duft, Death, Serpents-meat, Beaftly
Ware, *&c.* And this I will prove by the
Practice of each fort, *viz.* by both the Practice of the Chriftians, and the Practice of
the Quakers. And firft, the Chriftians they
read them in their Churches, practice them
in their Families, particularly the Lord's
Prayer, the Ten Commandments, the Apoftle's Creed, think themfelves, as Difciples of
Chrift, obliged to follow the Examples of the
Primitive Chriftians and Holy Martyrs, in
frequenting the Ordinances of Jefus Chrift,
as Baptifm, and the Lord's Supper, and divers other Commands, *&c.* They believe the
Scripture is given by divine Infpiration, and
infallibly true, being by Wife and Good Men
well expreffed and rightly applied, and that
                                                    the

the true Prophets speak truly ; so that there
is a sweet harmony in the Scriptures. They
believe also that *Moses* was the first Pen-man,
and divinely inspir'd, and his Writings quoted by Christ and his Aposties ; see *Mark*
12. 16. *Luke* 24. 27. *Luke* 16. 19. & 24. 27.
26,27,44. *Acts.*2. And for these and the like
Reasons they call it *Holy Scripture*.

But then, Secondly, if we must judge the
Tree by the Fruit, as Christ directed, then
the Quakers do not believe the Doctrin and
Precepts recorded in Scripture, to be either
blessed or holy, and *therefore* call them Dust,
Death, Husk, Serpents-meat, Beastly Ware *&c.*
which I thus prove :

First, By the very reproachful Language
and contemptuous Expression you cast upon
them, as Dust, Death, Serpents-meat, *&c.*

Secondly, In that you do not read them in
your Meetings for Worship, nor recommend
them to be read in your Monthly and Quarterly Meetings, as you frequently do your
own Epistles.

Thirdly, Because you say, That to preach
out of them is Conjuration, which you would
not, if you believed the Doctrines therein to
be holy and blessed.

Fourthly, By reason you lay aside as useless
the Use of the Lord's Prayer, Ten Commandments, and the Apostle's Creed, which
are some of those holy Precepts contained in
the Scriptures.

Fifthly, In that you deny the Ordinances
of *Jesus* Christ, and do not practise them ac-

D 4   cording

cording to the Command of Chrift, *Go teach all Nations, baptifing,* &c. *This do in remembrance of me,* &c. For if they were fincere, and did believe the Doctrin and Precepts were holy and bleffed, as they pretend, you would at fome time or other fee a Bible in their Hands, in a Meeting, and make Confeffion of Sin, and beg Pardon of God for Chrift's fake, which they never did.

Sixthly, That from your Practice, Words, and Writings you do prefer your own Books, Papers, and Epiftles before the Scriptures, as in *New* Rome *unmask'd,* &c. *New* Rome *arraign'd,* &c. For proof fee your Yearly Epiftle follows.

The 27th of the 3d Month, 1675.

'IT is our Sence, Advice, Admonition, and
' Judgment, in the Fear of God, and the
' Authority of his Power and Spirit, that no
' fuch *flight* and *contemptible* Names and Ex-
' preffions, as that faithful Friend's Papers,
' which we teftifie, hath been given out by
' the Spirit and Power of God, are Mens
' *Edicts* or *Canons,* &c. with fuch fcornful Say-
' ings, be *permitted* by *W. Penn, Alex. Packe,*
' *Stephen Crifp, George Whitehead,* and others.

Now I am apt to think, as fuperftitious as you are, that you did not afcribe Holinefs to the Paper and Ink of your own Papers and Pamphlets: But yet what Care, what Caution, what Advice and Admonition was fent out from the general Council, not of *Trent,* but *London,* that no fuch fcornful Expreffions fhould should be put upon your Friend's Papers, as *Edicts* and *Canons,* which indeed are not such contemptible Names? And yet how do you charge them, by the Authority of the Power and Spirit of God, that no such contemptible, scornful, and unsavory Expressions be permitted to be cast upon your Papers, which you say are given forth by the Power and Spirit of God ? So tender and careful you are of your own nonsensical Papers, Epistles, &c. Here is no calling them Death, Dust, Serpents-meat, Beastly Ware, Carnal Letter, Husk, and the like ; no, no, yours were given forth, you say, by the Power and Spirit of God ; and consequently the Doctrines contained in them (in your esteem) are blessed and holy ; and that is the reason why you are so tender and cautious of suffering any slight and contemptible Names and unsavory Expressions to be put upon them as *Mens Edicts.* But as for the Scripture, who knows, says you, whether *Moses* or *Hermes* was the first Pen-man ; or which part of Scripture was wrote so true, that we may depend on it, since, what the Prophets wrote is false, at least great part of it, and thereupon you who are thus doubtful do not believe the Doctrine and Precepts to be holy : And that doubtless is the Reason why you not only permit, but your selves, even the best of note amongst you, call the Scripture by such unsavory Names and contemptible Expressions, as Death, Dust, Serpents-meat, Beastly ware, &c. Again, by the care you take to spread your

Books

Books and Papers, and not the Scriptures, is self-evident that you do prefer your own Papers above the Scriptures. See your *Epiſt.*

Renewed Advice to the Monthly and Quarterly Meetings in England *and* Wales, *for ſpreading* Friends Books *for Truths Service,* Anno 1693.

Dear Friends,

HAving at ſeveral Yearly Meetings conſidered how all thoſe Books printed for the Service of Truth might moſt effectually be ſpread for a general Service to Truth ; ——That the Printer ſend to his Country Correſpondents, *&c.*

1. For Friends to have general notice what Books are printed, *&c.*

2. That they may ſend for what quantities they want.

3. That the Printer may be encourag'd in printing for Friends.

4. That one Book of a ſort may be kept in each Monthly and Quarterly Meeting.

Dear Friends, It's adviſed that ye be careful in *ſpreading all* ſuch Books writ in defence and for the ſervice of Truth, whether by way of Epiſtle, Caution, Warning, Exhortation, or Prophecy, that we may not be negligent in promoting Truth. Record this Epiſtle in your Quarterly Book, and ſometimes read it

for

for remembrance and notice. Signed on the
behalf of the Meeting, by *B. B.*

OBSERVATION.

Pray note, what Care, Caution, and Indu-
stry they use to spread their Books ; working
by Policy like Moles under ground, little taken notice of, until they turn up the Foundation. Here is not a Word of *Death, Dust,* or
Serpents-meat, Beastly Ware, &c. No, no ; nor not
a word of Scripture-Proof in either of these
Epistles. I was minded to put a Sample of
their Books and Epistles they write each to
the other, to be read in their Meetings, in one
Column ; and what they write to the World,
to decoy, in another Column ; shewing their
Books to be of two sorts, of two Stamps,
and to carry two Faces, as *G. W.* hath con-
fessed of *W. Smith's* Primer : One reads as *F. B.*
hath quoted ; another reads the contrary ;
and so is their general way. But I shall exceed what I at first intended.

See what Labour and Pains here is to
spread, disperse, and send up and down their
Books to all the Counties in *England* and
Wales. In the Yearly Epistle, *p.* 2. they tell
them, That in *Germany* their Books are dispersed, and Epistles recommended to *Barbadoes,
Maryland, Pensylvania, Virginia, Scotland, Hol-
land, Ireland* ; but not a word of recommen-
ding the Scripture : No, their Language and
Practice sufficiently discover their Disesteem
they

they have for it ; and their way, manner, and care to diſperſe their Erroneous Books, ſhould re-mind all good Chriſtians, and eſpecially Paſtours and Teachers, to aſſiſt in ſpreading ſuch Books as are, and have been wrote, to detect their Errors ; particularly Mr. *Norris*'s Book, and divers others. I ſhall conclude this, with ſhewing the Quakers way of charging their Diſciples to read their Epiſtles, *&c. Several Papers given forth for the ſpreading of Truth*, &c. *Viz.* ' I charge ' you in the Preſence of the Lord God, ' to ſend this [Epiſtle] amongſt all Friends ' and Brethren *every where*, to be read in all ' Meetings to you all ; *this* is the *Word* of ' God.   *Geo. Fox.*

Thus, like the Phariſees of old, they are making void the Holy Scripture by their Traditional Pamphlets, which they eſteem and prefer before Scripture ; as appears by undeniable Demonſtration, both from their Words and Practices, and which G. *W's* 12 Witneſſes may now perceive fairly proved.

The Fourth Charge againſt the
Quakers,

They deny the Ordinance of Jeſus Chriſt, as Baptiſm and the Lord's Supper.

THat they deny theſe two Ordinances, their Practices as well as their Doctrine
                    ſuffi-

fufficiently declare.   Yet in regard G. *W*. p. 2.
fays, ' As for Baptifm and the Lord's Supper,
' Scripturally confidered in their feveral Dif-
' penfations, in their Figure and Subftance,
' we confefs and own.   This is falfe, as their
Books declare, *viz.*

E. Burrough's *Works*, &c. *p.* 51. 'The
' Bread and Wine is vifible and carnal: ——
' We fee them : ——But a Carnal Figure of
' a Spiritual thing: ——The Figure is decla-
' red againft : ——For Chrift never fince he
' was Sacrificed brake of the Bread, or drank
' of the Cup with his Difciples, *p.* 581. we
' do deny, and do fay it is no Ordinance of
' God; neither was it ever commanded of
' him, or practifed by the Saints, but is an
' Inftitution of the Whore of *Rome*, and *Eng-*
' *land* received it by a Popifh Inftitution;
' and your Practice of it is Idolatry, and not
' any part of the true Worfhip of God. And
' as for your breaking Bread and drinking
' Wine, we do utterly deny to be of God.

News coming up, &c. ' A Voice and a Word
' to all you Deceivers and Blafphemers, who
' utter both your Blafphemy and Hypocrifie;
' that tell People of a Sacrament, and tell
' them 'tis the Ordinance of God. Blufh,
' blufh ; and tremble you who live in the
' Witchery, and bewitch the People, *&c.*

To the like purpofe fee *Smith's Primer,* p. 36.
and the *Mufick Lecture,* &c. *p.* 35. 'Where
' they are I was, *viz.* In Performances in Or-
' dinances, in Family-Duties, in Hearing in
                                        ' Read-

'Reading, in Prayers and Fafting : ——— but
'when I came to bend my Mind to that of
'God in me, I durft not give God Thanks
'for the Victuals fet before me, &c.

Obferve, Here is *E. B. G. Fox, Sol. Eccles,*
all great Prophets, and *W. Smith* one of their
Minifters, who teftifie both by Word and Doctrine, as well as the whole People by Practice, that it is no Ordinance of God, but an
Inftitution of the Whore of *Rome,* no part of
God's Worfhip, but abfolute Idolatry ; and
that fuch as tell People of a Sacrament, are
not only Witches, but Deceivers and Blafphemers, and ought not only to Blufh, but
Tremble, &c. And that though they had
been in the Obfervation , yet Quakerifm
hath fo alter'd their Judgment, as they confefs they have laid them afide. But ftill for
the Quakers thus to charge the Church of
England with a Popifh Inftitution, Idolatry,
&c. and yet feek to them for Favour, and a
kind Acceptation, 'tis prepofterous : So that I
might well fay, *How could you have the Face
to feek for Relief, till you retract thefe Errors.*
As to your Exception againft Sprinkling, and
feeming thereby to allow of Dipping : This
is fallacious, in that you practice neither.

F. B's

F. B's Fifth and Sixth Charge againft the 𝔔𝔲𝔞𝔨𝔢𝔯𝔰.

*That they undervalue the Death and Suf-
ferings of Chrift, and exalt their own
Sufferings above the Sufferings of Chrift,
above the Sufferings of the Apoftles,
above the Sufferings of the Martyrs, or
any Chriftians fince the days of Chrift,
&c.*

E. Burrow's *Works, &c.*

'And this is to go abroad into the Nati-
' on, and into the World : ——That
' the Sufferings of the People of God (called
' Quakers) in this Age, is greater Suffering,
' and more unjuft, than in the days of Chrift,
' or of the Apoftles, or in any time fince
' Queen *Mary*'s days, brought not forth a
' Suffering more cruel. ——What was done
' to Chrift, or the Apoftles, was chiefly done
' by a Law, and in great part by the due
' Execution of a Law, *&c.*

In my Sheet to the Parliament I put a
Query grounded upon this Doctrine, *viz.*
Whether was greateft, the Sufferings of the
Quakers, or the Sufferings of Chrift, to which
G. *W.* gave no direct Anfwer, but gloffed it
over, as his ufual way is : For if he had an-
fwered, that the Sufferings of the Quakers
had been greateft, as their Doctors Teach,
the

the People, would have been ready to stone him for Blasphemy. Again, if he had said, the Sufferings of Christ had been greatest, he had then given the Lie to *E. B.* their great Prophet: So that he was in a great Strait, like the Pharisees of old their Predecessors: For all the Saints Sufferings are not to be compared with the Sufferings of the ever-blessed Jesus. But in the next place, that they should thus exalt their own Sufferings above the Sufferings of the Apostles, Martyrs, *&c.* is such a boast, as hath no parallel amongst Protestants. But that is not all; they come in as Advocates for all the Tyrants and bloody Persecutors, who without any Law, and contrary to Law, martyr'd and murther'd many Thousands for Christ's sake, saying about six lines off, *And herein it appears the Sufferings to be more unjust, because what the Persecutors of old did to the People of God, they did by a Law, and by the due execution of a Law,* &c. So that to confute this grand Error, wicked Lye, and false Plea of the Quakers, first on behalf of the Persecutors, who they say executed their Cruelties upon the Apostles and Martyrs not only by a Law, but by the due execution of a Law: Next on the behalf of themselves; both which I shall consider distinctly, *viz.* The Sufferings of the Quakers of the one part, and the Sufferings of the Holy Apostles, Blessed Martyrs, and Pious Protestants, since the days of Christ, of the other part. I say, in order to confute this vain-glorious *Error,* I
shall

ſhall firſt produce a few Inſtances of the Sufferings of the Apoſtles and Martyrs, *&c.* and
next, a Sample or two of the *Quaker's Suffe-*
rings ; and let *G. W.* in his next ſhew his *Art,*
and deny my Argument if he can.

Firſt then, to begin with the Primitive
Sufferers, Apoſtles, and Bleſſed Martyrs, *viz.*
John Baptiſt, Stephen, James, Bartholomew,
Mark, Peter, Andrew, Matthew, Philip, Paul,
and divers others, ſome flead alive, ſome their
Brains knock'd out, ſome crucified, ſome burned alive ; what Law did theſe Worthies
ſuffer by ? Was the Law duly or juſtly executed upon them ? Anſwer in your next.

Secondly, What ſay you to the Ten Perſe-
cutions under thoſe bloody Tyrants, who,
as Hiſtory ſaith, ſuffered as many as amounted
to ſooo to a day, for 12 months together,
ſome rack'd, ſome burned, ſome drawn to
pieces by wild Horſes, ſome fryed, ſome
roaſted, ſome broiled upon Gridirons, ſome
melted Lead poured down their Throats,
ſome put into boiling Coppers of Oyl, ſome
rouled in Barrels of Nails, and a hundred
other exquiſite Tortures and barbarous Cruelties ; was this done by a Law, and the due
Executions of that Law ? And are your Sufferings greater ? Anſwer theſe three Queries
in your next, or elſe as *E. B.* ſaid, acknowledge under your Hands, That you have been
deceiv'd, and becomes falſe Witneſſes, and
publiſh your retractation, for thus deceiving
the World.

E . *Thirdly,*

3. What think you of the horrid Maſſacres in *France, Piedmont, Ireland,* and the Martyrdom of *Salter Badly, Thorp Hus, Jerom* of *Prague, Zuinglius, Calvin, Beza, Bilny, Bradford, Frith, Barns, Tindal, Ridley, Hooper,* Father *Latimer,* Dr. *Tayler,* Biſhop *Farrar,* and Archbiſhop *Cranmer* *, which in the whole, as from Hiſtory I can make appear, was more than 50000000, who ſuffered the like Tortures

* Which *W. P.* ſays, taught the *Papiſts* how to deal with the *Proteſtants,* by his Practice of Burning *Joan* of *Kent.*

which the Heathen Tyrants executed ; nay, uſed more or different Stratagems. Come *G. W.* in your next, anſwer the laſt three Queries directly, without ycur gloſſing or painting, for your Enchanting Art will not now do : For, 1*ſt,* Either theſe ſuffered by a Law, or they did not. 2*dly,* And by the due execution of that Law, or they did not. 3*dly,* That the Quakers Sufferings have been greater, or they have not. If the firſt, bring forth your Arguments to prove it, for I deny them jointly and ſeverally : If the laſt, are you not groſs Lyers and grand Impoſtors, who have the Impudence thus to impoſe upon the World ? Nay, 4*thly,* Are your Sufferings more cruel than the recited ? If not, you are found Falſe-witneſſes ; and your Verdict for and on the behalf of the due Proceedings and legal Executions of the bloody Tyrants, perſecuting Papiſts, and cruel Iriſh, will not paſs : You muſt go out again ; for

we

we say and deny that they suffered either by Law or the due execution of a Law ; or that your Sufferings were either *greater* or *more cruel* ; all which your Doctrine holds forth, and nothing will salve it, but an ingenuous Retractation, published in condemnation of *Burrough's* Doctrine, which is both taught, received, and believed by the poor misled Quakers. And now I shall proceed to shew a Sample of the Quakers Suffering, which being compared with the recited, the disproportion will the better appear, *viz.* For *Meeting*, for *Not Swearing*, for *wearing the Hat*, for *Tithes* and *Church-Dues, &c.* from 1650. the day of the Quakers date, to 1658. which was after *E. Burrough* had wrote the Book above recited, which was in 1657. though I grant it was reprinted in 1672. *viz.*

A Declaration of the present Sufferings, &c.

J. Evans imprison'd for speaking to a Priest.
J. Norris of *Swasy*, for the same.
El. Fowler speaking in Steeple-house prison'd.
J. Green of *Bulbrook*, for the like
John Rogers imprison'd for the like.
Ann Blackling at *Bury*, for the like.
George Harrison, for meeting, was abused till he did spit Blood.
Bar. Logg fin'd 3 *s.* 4 *d.* for his Hat.
Tho. Bagg, for not putting off his Hat, and for not swearing, was fined 13 *s.* 4 *d.*

Reader, here is one Sample of the *Quakers* Sufferings, which they bring in competition; nay, fay they exceed all before them since the days of Chrift : But what was it for? namely, for disturbing the exercise of the eftablish'd Religion.   But if any now disturb them, let them look for worfe Sufferings, not putting off their Hats, *&c.*   For mark :   As they cannot for Confcience fake put off their Hats to their Superiors, no more can they fuffer their Inferiors to ftand with their Hats on ; witnefs their forcing their Apprentices to ftand bare-headed before them : And likewife for meeting together.   And for that the Poor Man was fo abufed, that he did fpit blood :   Ay, that he did, and 'tis recorded a Suffering too, to help to make up the balance between the Sufferings of the *Quakers* of the one part, and the Sufferings of Chrift, his Apoftles and Martyrs on the other part. Pray fee the other Sample. .

The Record of Sufferings for Tythes.

	£	s	d
W. Ground's Tythes 2s. took a Mare,	5	o	o
W. Ground's Wardens, Rate 2 *s.* 1 *d.*			
a Kettle,	o	10	o
R. Letchworth, Tythes 20 *s.* 2 Cows,	5	o	o
Dan. Pechy, for Tythes 2 doz. Yarn,	o	2	o
Rob. Crabb, Tythes 1 *s.* 1 *d.* took a Kettle,	o	7	o
Cl. Crabb, for Dues 7 *s.* Pot of Butter,	1	o	o
Hen. Place, dues 1 *s.* 6 *d.* took Goods	o	3	o

W. Johu-

W. Johnson, Tythes 9 *s.* 10*d.* Pot Butt. 1   3   0
R. Crabb 2 Wardens, Rates 1 *s.* 10 *d.*
   took Goods,   0   4   10
El. Carecroft , Clerk's Wages 2 *d.*
   took Goods,   0   0   8
Another time, for the Popish Stee-
   ple houfe,   0   1   0
Sam. Cater, dues 10 *d.* took a Kettle, 0   5   0

Reader, I have given you a large Sample both of what they fuffer'd and what they took beyond what was due, as they fay, at their own price, and yet forced to bring in 8 *d.* and 12 *d.* Sufferers ; and yet it will not balance for the whole fum of their Sufferings in eight years time through *England* and *Wales,* in Pots and Kettles, Dripping-pans, Candlefticks, Pans, Barrels, Difhes, Cart-wheels, and other Lumber, comes to but 1568 *l.* 14 *s.* 8 *d.*

Behold the difproportion ; and yet they are not afhamed; no, they are not at all afhamed : But if they have any fhame in them, I intend to make them afhamed ; and in order to it, let me give you *Cater,* one of their Praters, I fhould have faid Preachers, fince he is fo upon Record, who formerly was a poor Journeyman *Carpenter,* with his Budget of Tools at his Back ; but fince he got the knack of Preaching worth many hun-dreds, *&c.* and I prefume much of it got this way, *viz.*

'*Sam. Cater,* for being at a Meeting at *Phackenham* in *Norfolk,* the 4th. of the 5th.
           E 3   Month,

'Month, 1670. preaching and publishing the
'Gospel of Peace, one *Ann Wats,* a Woman-
'Informer, told the Officers, who came with
'a Warrant, and had him before *Christopher*
'*Colthorp* a Justice, who fined him 20 *l.* which
'Warrant and Conviction he sent to the
'Justices of the Isle of *Ely,* namely, *John La-*
'*ney, Henry Hitch,* and *Thomas March,* who in
'pursuance of the *Norfolk* Justice's Convicti-
'on, sent their Warrant to the Officers of
'*Littleport* (in the Isle of *Ely*) who distrai-
'ned as much Houshold-stuff and Timber
'from the said *S. Cater* as was worth more
'than 20 *l.*

Reader, this is a Copy of the Record of
their Quarterly Book, unless they have torn
it out for madness since I have discover'd the
Cheat, who stands Recorded a Sufferer above
20 *l.* for preaching, when in truth he did not
suffer 20 *d.* Nay, he was so far from that,
that he got 10 *l.* clear by it. And yet 100
year hence, when all are dead that know the
matter, and none able to contradict it, it
will look like a noble and valiant Act in *S. C.*
thus to preach, and thus to suffer for preaching. And perceiving by their last yearly
Epistle, that they keep to their old way of
sending up to *London* their Sufferings from
those Quarterly and Monthly Meetings, I am
the willinger to shew the nature of their Sufferings, and the manner of their Proceedings,
and particularly about Tythes taken from
them, whether the Real Value due by Law,

or

or two or three times the Value : So that
when their faithful Chronicles come forth,
which they have told us of this 20 years, such
as have been moderate, and for ease to the
Quakers and themselves, have taken no more
than the Real Value, nay, 'perhaps less, shall
be render'd *Persecutors* in the next Age.

Epist. p. 1. ' That Friends, at all Monthly
' and Quarterly Meetings, call for the Suffe-
' rings of Friends, to see that they be sent
' up (to *London*) both of what Tythes are
' pretended to be due, and for how long
' time, and the time when taken, and by and
' for whom, and what Goods are taken, and
' the value thereof ; as well of those not ex-
' ceeding as those exceeding the sums deman-
' ded, both being a Suffering for Truths sake ;
' they being in these Particulars found de-
' fective, is an Obstruction to the general
' Record of Friends Sufferings : And there-
' fore the Monthly and Quarterly Meetings
' are advised to take more Care for the fu-
' ture, that all Friends Sufferings for Truths
' sake may be brought up as full and com-
' pleat in all respects as may be, *&c.*

By which 'tis evident that they design to
represent to the next Age all Persons who
take Tythes, let them be never so moderate
in their Demands and taking of Tythes,
Persecuters : Which as it is an ill Representa-
tion for such a Nation as this, who profess
the Name of Jesus, so is it both uncharitable
and ungrateful in them, their Indulgence con-

sider'd.

fider'd. And that they do fo intend, fee their Book, *Judas and the Jews, &c.* p. 41. ' Our ' Faithful Chronicles of the bloody Trage- ' dies of that Profeffing Generation, will tell ' future Ages other things, *&c.* From which paffage three things are obfervable : '1ft, *That Profeffing Generation,* meaning the *Presbyterians, Independants,* and *Baptifts,* for they do account them *Profeffors of Chrift,* but not *Poffeffors* or *Enjoyers* of what they profefs, only empty *Profeffors,* meer *Notionifts,* airy *Talkers, &c.* 2. But the *Epifcopalians* they account the Pro- phane, the Publicans, the Vulgar or Com- mon People, but both of the World ; and their Teachers falfe, their Scriptures Death, their Gofpel Duft and Serpents-meat, their Ordinances an Inftitution of the Whore, and rejected by themfelves. 3. But themfelves the *only Poffeffors* and *Enjoyers* of the Light, Spirit, and Subftance, together with a few pious Gentiles, as *G. W.* calls them in his Book, *The Chriftian Doctrine, &c.* p. 9. And *W. Penn* beftows about 40 Pages in folio upon Gentile Divinity, in his *Chrift. Quak.&c.* Yea, *Ellwood, Richardfon,* and the moft Learned amongft them, as they have fhewed all the Contempt they can to *Jefus of Nazareth,* (calling him a Veil, a Garment, which they can never call Chrift) to the *Scriptures,* to the *Ordinances* and *Minifters* of Jefus of *Naz.* with great Incharity : So on the other hand they have taken all the care they can to raife the Fame of the Gentiles, Heathens, Jewifh Ido- laters,

laters, as possibly afterwards may be made appear. Well, but this is a Digreffion, let us come to *Sam. Cater's* Sufferings.

First, 'tis true he did preach, was fined, was distrained, as recorded, but all his Goods was returned, and for this Noble Act he had 10 *l.* sent him out of the Treasury from *London*, by *John Peacock,* late of St. *Ives,* as a Recompence ; but his poor Neighbors *R. Crabb, T. Paine,* and others, was fined and distrained for meeting *June* 9. 1670. and neither had their Goods again, nor a Reward out of *London* Chest, that I ever heard. A notable way to encourage such Praters to banter all other Diffenters (who are not so vainglorious as themselves, nor so cunning and close as the Quakers, who may compare with Jesuit and Jew) as *G. W.* in his *Christ. Quak. and Dev.* did, who charged them to hold *Erroneous and Blasphemous Principles, carnal Policy, timerous, creeping, occult, cowardly, base,* &c. And as I said, that I may make them ashamed of their deceitful Practices, who thus banter and domineer over all other People, I may recite part of an Edict, (only I must remember not to give their Laws such contemptible Names as Edicts) which enjoined the *Hearers* to meet constantly, and suffer greatly, insomuch as that in the loss of 1355.0 *l.* their Preachers never lost 50 *l.* And the Reasons thereof are more *particularly* handled in my Book, *The painted Harlot both stripp'd and whipp'd,* &c.

An

An Abſtract of their Antimagiſtratical Edict is as followeth, *viz.*

London, 27. of the 3d Month, 1675.

IT is our Advice and Judgment, That all Friends keep up thoſe publick Teſtimonies, and neither decline, forſake, nor remove their publick Aſſemblies, becauſe of Times of Sufferings, as worldly, fearful, and politick Profeſſors have done, &c. *Signed by* G. W. W. P. *and divers others.*

Yet notwithſtanding how did G. *Whitehead* creep up and down, here and there, with all the caution and timeroufneſs poſſible? to evince which, ſee a Letter he order'd to be writ to me, to appoint a Meeting for him, &c.

D *Ear Friend F. B.* G. W. *is now here, and doth purpoſe to be at your Meeting the* 27th *Inſtant, and therefore deſireth that Friends may be together by the* 11th *hour at furtheſt. Thou need not mention his Name to any particularly, but maiſt acquaint them of a Friend's Intention to be with them the time aforeſaid. So with* G. W'*s dear Love to thee and thy Wife, I reſt thy dear Friend,*

Stoake, 25th of the   John
11th Mon. 1675.   Hen. Hubbard, *jun.*

Thus wary was G. *W.* and cautious in his Travels, which had been well enough, had
he

he left the People free : But for him to make
a Law against the National Law, that they
must constantly meet, and neither forsake, remove, nor decline, *&c.* like worldly, politick
and fearful Professors, yea, antiscriptural too;
For, said Christ, *if they persecute you in one city,
flee or remove to the next.* And his inspired
Disciples oftentimes met privately for fear of
the Jews, *&c.* yet how did *G. W.* like *Abab*
go disguised ? he must not be known, his
Name must not be mentioned.

Well, I knew him and his Name too, and
had his Company and dear Love too, and
called Dear Friend, yea, all dear to me at
that time, though now I have so disturbed
this subtile Fox, and so manifested his deceitful Practices in many things, that he cannot
afford me my proper Name, only *Bugg* ; *Bugg*
say so ? *Bugg* quote, *&c. Bugg* 's Testimony; yea
34 times he calls me only *Bugg* in one Sheet ;
and since I came to *London,* in a private Letter, in one side of half a sheet, he calls me
eleven times only *Bugg,* such is his proud,
disdainful, and insolent Behaviour, besides
scurrilous Names and *reproachful Terms,* far.
contrary to their pretence in the beginning.
See,

An Account of the Children of Light, &c.
p. 16. ' Also it hath been laid upon us by the
' Lord, to call Men and Women by their
' Names, which their Fathers have given
' them to be known amongst Men by, *&c.*

But

But *G. W.* is grown so great since he came
first amongst the *Quakers, Anno* 1652. (a
poor Boy about 15 or 16 years old, travel-
ling on foot) and hath so gathered up his
Crumbs, though chiefly at other Mens Ta-
bles, that he scorns to call him that hath fed
him and his Friends at his Table by his proper Name : Oh, Insolent and Imperious
George !

I have been the longer on this Head, because 'tis the most glorious Jewel in their
Crown, how counterfeit soever it be within : For, when there was no Persecution,
they cut themselves out Work, by disturbing of Churches, for which they sometimes suffer'd the Justice due to such Offen-
ders, and then they cried out of Persecution, and resolved to go on against all Law,
Government, and Rule, and all that oppo-
sed them : herein was *Nebuchadnezzar, Da-
rius, &c.* and themselves *Daniel, Shadrack,&c.*
and in a little time came to collect their Sufferings, whether it was 6 *d.* 8 *d.* or 1 *s.* in it
went ; and having by 1657. in *England* and
Wales, muster'd up 1568 *l.* 14 s. 8 *d.* they
printed, and taught, That their Sufferings
was *greater* and *more unjust* than the Sufferings of Christ, his Apostles, and Martyrs,
and *more unjust* in that they suffered by a
Law, and that Law duly executed. I do
not doubt, but if *G. F's* Works be printed,
there will be such a discovery of *Quakerism* as
the World never saw ; but I do declare my

Be-

Belief is, they will never print them, left
they be laid by *Sol. Eccles* Fiddles : Possibly
they may print some Passages of his Travels,
to make Fools admire , and Wise Men
laugh.

VI *Charges against* G. W.

I. **A** 𝕻𝖚𝖇𝖑𝖎𝖈𝖐 𝕯𝖊𝖋𝖆𝖒𝖊𝖗. See his Book
Judgment fixed, &c. p. 263. " Fran-
" cis Bugg *is turned Informer* : To let pass all
his other Names, as *Canker'd Apostate, Vile
Apostate, Self-condemn'd Apostate,* Judas *Runa-
gate, Beast, Dog, Wolf, Child of the Devil, Ene-
my of all Righteousness, &c.* That very Name
Informer, the time 1682. consider'd, is suffi-
cient to term and prove him a publick Defamer, and a malicious Incendiary ; for he
knew me to be no such manner of Person,
but one of the greatest *Sufferers by Informers*
in the whole County. But however *T. Bird,
J. Mason, J. Ellington, W. Belslam,* and above
Twenty more Quakers, gave me a Certificate, to certifie the contrary ; and did very
nobly testifie against such Antichristian
Treatment. But it is by such Arts they have
raised their Structure, witness their Book entituled, *A Battledoor, &c.* saying *p.* 3. *Come ye
Doctors, Scholars, Teachers, and Magistrates, &c.*
in

in which, befide the *Englifh,* and fome other
foreign Languages, there was thè *Latin, Ita-
lian, Greek, Hebrew, Chaldee,* and *Syriack* ; and
before each of thefe Six Languages, in each
Page, at the beginning of each Language,
they erected the form and figure of a Child's
Penny horning Battledoor, fubfcribed on the
Handle thereof *Geo. Fox* ; and all was about
Thee and *Thou, fingular* and *plural,* as if they
had been fuch *Ignoramuffes* as did not under-
ftand *tu* and *vos,* without the help of *Geo. Fox,*
who was, before a Quaker, a poor Journeyman Shoemaker. But it was a notable Pro-
ject to bring both Learning and the Learned
into Contempt, to the fcandal òf the *Englifh*
Nation : Thus defamatory have their Libels
been. The next Book this Imperious *Fox*
provided for the Clergy, was entituled, *A
Primmer for all the Doctors and Scholars in* Europe, but efpecially *Oxford* and *Cambridge,*
containing 2434 Queries of this import, *viz.*
What is a *Verb,* a *Participle,* an *Adverb,* a *Ge-
tive Cafe,* &c. what is the word called *decli-
ned* ; who was the firft Author of it, and by
whom it came, *&c.* And with the greateft
Contempt and Reproach, conceivable, as by
his lofty Strains, bold Challenges, and daring
Interrogations, with which thé faid Primmer
is plentifully ftuft, doth appear, faying,

‘ Thefe Queries are to call you out into the
‘ Field ; the little *Davids* are rifen, who have
‘ the Baggs, the Slings, and the Stones : Ye
‘ that profefs your felves wife and learned
‘ Men,

' Men, and are Novices and Fools, answer
' me ; draw out your Weapons if you have
' any, and answer me these things : Come
' out of your Holes, and do not skip nor hip
' from them ; answer every Word in particu-
' lar, for you have Tongue enough some-
' times, let us see now if it can wagg, *&c.*
' ———G. *Fox.* For more of this impertinent
Nonsense see my Book, *Battering Rams against*
New Rome. Thus scandalous and defamatory have they been in their contemptuous
Libels against both the Gentry and Clergy of
the English Nation, on purpose to raise themselves out of their Ruins ; [for they had no
better way to prove their own Religion true,
than by rendring all others false.] But when
these Libels and pernicious Books would not
do their business fully, then they termed them
False Prophets, Deceivers, *&c.* See their Book
A brief Discovery of a threefold Estate, &c.
p. 7, 8, 9, 10. *viz.* ' The Priests of the World
' are, 1. Conjurers, raising dead Doctrines out
' of the Letter which is Death, raising Death
' out of Death ; notable Conjurers. 2. Thieves
' and Robbers. 3. Antichristians. 4. Witches.
' 5. Devils. 6. Lyars,——— The Commission
' and Call of *Baal's* Priests, came from *Ox-*
' *ford* and *Cambridge.* 7. A Viperous and Ser-
' pentine Generation. 8. Blasphemers. 9. Scar-
' let-coloured Beasts. 10. *Babylon's* Merchants,
' selling Beastly Wares, ——— the Letter,
' which is Dust and Death. 11. Whited
' Walls. 12. Ravening Wolves. 13. Greedy
' Dogs,

'Dogs, — Really they are Bloudhounds ſtill
'hunting and gaſping after their Prey, like
'the Mouth of Hell : Wo, wo, wo was
'the Portions of thoſe Phariſees then, and
'wo, wo, wo is their Portion now ; and Wo
'and Miſery is the Portion of the Upholders
'(*i. e.* Parliament) of that Treacherous Crew
'and deceitful Generation, *&c.*

Come G. *W.* anſwer in your next, whether
your diſperſing theſe Defamatory Libels unlicens'd be not ſeditious, ſcandalous, and tend
to the ſcandal of the Clergy, Parliament, and
People ; and yet they forgive you all your
Treſpaſſes, paſs by your many Affronts :
But you, like the wicked Servant, whom his
Lord forgave all for a Trifle, fall upon others.
But you will ſay, this was in *Oliver's* time ;
Why ? Was *Oxford* and *Cambridge* a Nurſery
for-*Baal's* Prieſts in *Oliver's* time ? And is it
otherwiſe now ? No, you are the ſame you
were : See your Book, *The Guide miſtaken,*
p. 18. printed 1668. by *W. Penn.* 'And
'whilſt the idle Gormondizing Prieſts of En-
'gland, run away with above 150000 pounds
'a year, under pretence of being God's Mi-
'niſters, —— And that no ſort of People
'have been ſo univerſally, through Ages, the
'very bane of Soul and Body of the Uni-
'verſe, as that Abominable Tribe, for whom
'the Theatre of God's moſt dreadful Ven-
'geance is reſerved, to act their Eternal Tra-
'gedy upon.

Rea-

Reader, I hope by this time I have not only proved G. *W.* a Publick Defamer, but alſo his Brethren the like.

II. **A Wicked Forger.** The *Vind. &c.* *p. 3. Fra. Bugg* affirms in his Book *de Chr. Lib. par. 2. p.* 83 printed 1682. that Conformity is a Monſter, *&c.* —— and about two years after *he himſelf* conform'd, *&c.* In anſwer, I am not the Author of one word of that Page, but the whole Paſſage is a Query of *John Ainſloes,* propounded to *S. Cater* and others, beginning *p.* 81. ending *p.* 87. with his Name to it, and by me quoted as his ſence touching that Conformity they requir'd of him, about taking his Wife in ſubjection to their Law of Womens Meetings, and to whom neither *J. Ainſloe* nor my ſelf ever conformed : And as it was *J. A*'s, and by me quoted, to ſhew his ſence, and to manifeſt Quakers againſt Quakers, ſo it's an abſolute piece of Forgery to ſay, he affirms *he himſelf* conformed, ——his own Teſtimony : When all this while it was none of *F. B.* but *J. H*'s writing, and both his Name and Date, with a black line drawn to diſtinguiſh it from mine. Who then can give credit to this Inſincere, pretended ſerious G. *W.* this grand Forger.

III. **A Wilful Lyar.** *The Content. Apoſtate, &c. p. 3.* ' F. *Bugg* and his Company ' being got to the Meeting before G. *W.* and ' into the Gallery where our Miniſtring ' Friends uſed to be, *&c.* In ſhort, 'tis falſe, and that to G. *Whitehead*'s Knowledge too;

for

for there was not a Man of my Company in the Gallery with me, but *S. Cater* ; and this he wilfully and malicioufly fent abroad, to render me a turbulent Difturber ; which is fully proved in *New Rome unm. &c.* p. 50, 51.

IV. **A Grofs Perverter.** *The Quakers Vind. &c.* p. 3. ‘ Note, that the Inftances *Bugg*
‘ has to prove the Quaker’s Contempt of Go-
‘ vernors, being between the years 1654. and
‘ 1659.——when ’tis clear (thereby) that
‘ the Magiftrates and Minifters inftanced
‘ were thofe very Perfecuters and Ufurpers in
‘ *O. Cromwel’s* days, whereby *F. B.* has at once
‘ juftified thofe Magiftrates or Governors in
‘ thofe days, as Chrift’s Magiftrates, and con-
‘ fequently the Ufurpation of that Govern-
‘ ment teftified againft by *E. B.* and others.
Reader, the main thing intended by this Per-
verter *G. W.* is to make the World believe that they were fuch Enemies to *Oliver* and his Ufurpation, as that *E. Burr.* and the Quakers only reprehended thofe Governours and Magiftrates as fuch, when ’tis no fuch mat-
ter ; for tho’ I grant they were wrote in *O.C*’s time, yet they were reprinted in 1672. and by the Quakers common confent and appro-
bation, and for which they are refponfible until they condemn them. Well, but did *G. Fox, E. Burrough* fo feverely reprehend that Ufurpation ? I do think, who ever read *The Quakers unmafk’d, &c.* will be of another mind. P. 21. *To all you who are called Delinquents and Cavaliers :* ‘ Thus faith the Lord, My Con-
　　　　　　　　　　　　　　‘ troverfie

' troverſie is againſt you, even my Hand of
' Judgment is upon you already, and you are
' become curſed in all your hatchings.—And
' though your Kings, and Princes, and Nobles
' have been cut off in Wrath,—yet you re-
' pent not ; nor will you ſee how you are gi-
' ven up to be a Curſe, and a Deſolation, and
' a Prey in Houſes, and Lands, and Perſons to
' them whom I raiſed up (*i. e. O. Cromwel*)
' againſt you, and gave Power over you.——
' And you and your Kings and Lordly Power
' ſhall be enſlaved by the Devil in the pit of
' Darkneſs, in everlaſting Bondage, where he
' ſhall reign your Lord and King for ever-
' more, *&c.* Given under my Hand and ſea-
' led by the Spirit of the Eternal God, through
' *Edw. Burrough.* Taken at firſt out of the
Trumpet of the Lord ſounded, *p. 9.* but left
out of *E. B's* Works in the reprint, which ar-
gues, that *G. W. &c.* did not believe *E. Burr.*
was ſo moved, nor that his Meſſage was ſo
ſealed by the Eternal God, as *E. B.* pretended,
for if they did, they dealt very unfaithfully to
leave out ſuch a notable Prophecy.

Thus you ſee *E. Burrough* was ſo far from
reprehending *Oliver* or his Uſurpation, that
he tells what the Delinquents was, and how
God's Hand was upon the Royal Party, their
Kings, Princes, Nobles, Lands, Houſes, *&c.*
in Judgment; and that *Oliver* was raiſed of
God, *&c.* Well, let us hear what *G. R.* another of their Prophets ſays, *viz.*

' T

' TO thee, O. *Cromwel*, thus faith the Lord,
' I have chofen thee amongft the thou-
' fand of the Nations, to execute my Wrath
' upon my Enemies, and gave them to thy
' Sword, with which I fought for the Zeal of
' my own Name, and gave thee the Enemies
' of my own Seed to be a Curfe and a Re-
' proach for ever ; and many have I cut
' down by my Sword in thy Hand, that my
' Wrath might be executed upon them to the
' utmoft. *The Righteoufnefs of God, &c.* p. 11.
Geo. Rofe.

Come G. *W.* was this reprehending O.C. or
his Government ?   Are you not alhamed to
give occafion thus to difcover your corrupt
Principles by your bafe Pervertions ? Well,
hear G. Fox, *To the Parliament of the Common-
wealth, &c.* p. 8. ' Let all thefe Abby-Lands,
' Gleab-Lands, that's given to the Priefts, be
' given to the Poor of the Nation ; and let
' all the great Houfes, Abbies, Steeple-houfes,
' and *White-hall*, be for Alms-houfes.

Come G. *W.* what Paint have you in ftore
to falve thefe your grand Pervertions, horri-
ble Principles, and new Forgeries, and falfe
Gloffes ? What ! did you think your Sheet
would never be anfwer'd ?   Well *George*, I
have not done, but having retrieved my Head
from the Wall, by acquitting my felf from ju-
ftifying O. *C*'s Ufurpation, and alfo pointed
to the very Creatures, Flatterers, and Prophets
who

who both juftified, abetted, encourag'd, and
affented to the faid Ufurpation. See *The Quakers unmask'd, &c.* I am now coming to tell
you what Ufurpation I am againft, *viz.*

The Ufurpation of the Quakers.

And that in divers refpects ; firft, In that
you fummons the King's Subjects to meet
annually in *London,* by way of general Council or Convocation, without any legal Warrant, Writ, or other legal Authority : And
when fate in Councel in *Devonfhire-houfe* you
make Laws, Edicts, and Canons for the King's
Subjects throughout *England* to obferve, contrary and in direct oppofition to thofe very
Laws, Rules, *&c.* which the King and Parliament make at *Weftminfter.* This is the
Ufurpation I am againft, if you would needs
know of me what I account Ufurpation :
And that you have done fo, fee your yearly
Epiftle, *May* 1675. where, in oppofition to
the Law the King and Parliament made, that
you fhould not meet above Four, *&c.* you
in oppofition made a Law, That your People fhould neither forfake, decline, nor remove their Meeting. This was one remar-
kable Inftance of your juftling with Authority, and of your fetting your ufurping Poft
by the legal Poft ; and a Hundred Inftances
more of your arbitrary illegal Proceedings
and Ufurpations might be brought. But to
mention a few frefh Inftances, fee your laft
yearly

yearly Epiftle, entituled, *The Epiftle to the Monthly and Quarterly Meetings in* England *and* Wales, *and elfewhere, from our Yearly Meeting held in* London *the* 5, 6, 7, 8. *days of the 4th Month,* 1693 in which, amongft other things, you *p.* 3. order.

1. That your Books be fpread up and down the Nation as well as in parts beyond the Seas, which being unlicens'd, and tending to defame both the Clergy and Gentry, is a Ufurpation I am againft.

2. That none fhould pay Tythes, but refufe payment thereof, as an Antichriftian Yoke of Bondage; which fhew that you at *Devonfhire-houfe* interfere with thofe at *Weftminfter.*

3. That none fhould pay to the Steeplehoufe Rates or Leys, which put the Country to great trouble, and your Profelytes, who fubmit their Necks to your Ufurpation to great Sufferings, tending to Sedition and very evil Effects.

4. *That none fhould carry Guns in their Ships.* This fhews that you are not content with your own Eafe, but as far as your Ufurpation prevail, you weaken the Government, and are not willing to leave your People [your People, did I fay? yes, your People; for if you fay once what they fhall or fhall not do, 'tis a Law like that of the *Meads, &c.*] to their Freedom in this and many other Inftances, 1. Whether to publifh their Intentions to marry before Womens Meetings or not. 2. To

meet

meet preciſely at the time, day, and place, whether the Law command the contrary or not. 3. To pay Tythes, or not. 4. To pay to the Church Rates or not. 5. To carry Guns, and ſerve their King and Country, or not. 6. To buy of your Books, as they are perſwaded, concerning the Truth of them or not. I ſay, Did you leave your People free, and at liberty in theſe and other things, you would do well: Then if any particular perſon could not for Conſcience ſake acquieſce in any of theſe things, wherein the Law requires their active Obedience; then let ſuch pray the Magiſtrates and Government to hold them excus'd, and when ſo done, let them acknowledge the Favour from the Government, who only ought to be Judges in that Caſe. But your taking upon you this Uſurped Dominion, the more you prevail upon the People, the leſs the Kingdom is, and conſequently the more you encreaſe, the more dangerous. And this Uſurpation I teſtified againſt in my Book *de Chr. libertate, Anno* 1682. and in *Painted Harlot, &c.* 1683. and in ſeveral other Books; and now you ſee I am of the ſame Judgment ſtill touching Uſurpation, *&c.*

V. **A Falſe Gloſſer.** *The Qua. Vind. &c. p* 2. *F. B. accuſes ſomebody with objecting againſt paying Tythes under the new Covenant, becauſe abrogated by Chriſt, obſerving from thence, that the Quakers condemn the Martyrs,* &c. Obſerve this Falſe Gloſſer: I did not ſay they condemn either Martyr or others, who did refuſe payment of Tythes; I neither ſaid ſo, nor will my

my words carry any such intendment, but by
that Doctrine laid down by *Tho. Ellwood,* in
his *Antidote, &c. p.* 78. ' Truth allows no pay-
' ment of Tythes at all under the new Cove-
' nant ; they who pay Tythes uphold a legal
' Ceremony abrogated by Chrift, and thereby
' deny Chrift come in the Flefh, which is a
. ' Mark of Antichrift, *&c.* I fay, by this Doctrine they do conclude, That all that pay
Tythes, whether voluntary or by force, and
all fuch as receive Tythes, and make Laws that
Tythes fhall be paid, are Antichriftians; nay,
not only the prefent Generation of Men, but
all former and future Generations that have
been, or fhall be, fince the days of Chrift being perfonally on Earth to the Worlds end :
And 'tis this your Incharity that I oppofe, and
think it great prefumption in you to feek Favour at the hands of fuch as you condemn as
Antichriftians, *&c.*

VI. **A Deceiver of the People.** See *Judg-
ment fix'd, Introd. &c. If the Lord did not lay a Necessity
upon me, I should chufe to be mute ; —but the Lord has laid
the Necessity upon me.* — *I neither confult Events nor fear
Effects,* &c. If what I have herein faid be true, and which
I offer to prove before 10 or 12 impartial Men, then he
is a great Deceiver of the People ; nay, were it needful,
where I have mentioned one Prefident, (which in order to
prove my Charge I was obliged to do) I could have mention'd ten, both Lyes, Perverfions, Forgeries, Falfe Gloffes, and fcandalous Defamations, both of my felf and others.
But this may ferve for both Caution and Warning to fuch
as, like the noble *Bereans* of old, are willing to try all
things : Which that they may, is the hearty Defire of him
that was once *led away* by their Diffimulation.

Fra. Bugg.